IT'S NOT THAT
I'M BITTER...

IT'S NOT THAT I'M BITTER...

Or How I Learned

to Stop Worrying About

Visible Panty Lines

and Conquered the World

GINA BARRECA

ST. MARTIN'S PRESS ⚹ NEW YORK

IT'S NOT THAT I'M BITTER . . . Copyright © 2009 by Gina Barreca. All rights
reserved. Printed in the United States of America. For information, address St.
Martin's Press, 175 Fifth Avenue, New York, N.Y. 10010.

www.stmartins.com

Library of Congress Cataloging-in-Publication Data

Barreca, Regina.
    It's not that I'm bitter— : or how I learned to stop worrying about visible panty
lines and conquered the world / Gina Barreca.—1st ed.
        p. cm.
    ISBN-13: 978-0-312-54726-4
    ISBN-10: 0-312-54726-9
    1. Women—Psychology—Humor.   2. Women—Attitudes—Humor.   I. Title.
    HQ1206.B2727 2009
    155.6'33—dc22

                                                            2009003786

First Edition: May 2009

10   9   8   7   6   5   4   3   2   1

For *Fay Weldon,* C.B.E., whose poignant instructions on authorship remain the best advice for writers everywhere: "Gina," she announced when I was twenty-nine and couldn't afford a pair of red shoes in the window of Bergdorf's, "you must write books that people will *read*."

In the hope that this will be one of those books, *It's Not That I'm Bitter* . . . is dedicated with admiration and affection to Fay.

Contents

Contents

Contents

Contents

Acknowledgments

This is Michael Flamini's book.

Sure, I supplied the pages, and all mistakes and tacky lines are mine, but since the book itself wouldn't exist without The Extraordinary Flamini, his name should be on the cover. For those of you who don't get out a lot, Michael is the Executive Editor at St. Martin's Press, a dashing knight in a Paul Stuart suit who knows food, wine, Paris, films, Sondheim lyrics, seventies kitsch, *The Sopranos,* and what's funny. When Michael said my commentary on bathing suit season at T.J. Maxx was a riot, I finally knew for a fact that it was. Working with Michael was a piece of cake. Or a plate of profiteroles, to be more precise. It was, in other words, perfection.

Vicki Lame, Glorious Assistant Editor (and I believe that is her official title), made the day-to-day asking of panicky questions

("What's the minimum word count?!" and then, a few weeks later, "What's the maximum word count?!") a breeze, and was herself an encouraging and supportive presence throughout the creation of the manuscript; she deserves thanks and applause.

Copy editor Barbara Wild humbled my English Professor self: She caught my lapses in grammar, style, and judgment. I am grateful for her meticulous review of the manuscript.

My own assistants at the University of Connecticut, less officially editorial but also glorious, appear in their own right in several of the essays. Nevertheless, I want to thank them right up front: Without the brilliant Sarah McIntyre, Melissa Mullins, the fabulous Karen Renner, Amanda Smith, Sam Buzzelli, and Morgan Bowman, I would have chewed more fingernails, wrecked more computer files, and spent more nights agonizing over organization. I also would have written less well, laughed less often, and been far less productive. I owe you.

To the editors who inspired, read, worked on, and published versions of some of these pieces in other forms and formats, my humble and profound thanks: John Timpane of *The Philadelphia Inquirer,* Alex Kafka and Liz Macmillan of *The Chronicle of Higher Education,* Daniel Born of *The Common Review,* Carolyn Lumsden of *The Hartford Courant,* Jay Heinrichs of *Spirit* magazine, Ellen DeLisio of *Education World,* and Bob Sullivan of *LIFE* all have my sincere gratitude.

Friends and colleagues know what they mean to me: Gene Weingarten remains the smartest and funniest writer I know (just don't tell him) and inspires me; Pam Katz and her daughters, Rebecca and Louisa Ballhaus, reminded me why life is funny and—as a writer herself—Pam kept me going; another writer, Maggie Mitchell, who has ushered me through earlier books, kept believing that this one, too, would materialize, a la Rumpelstilskin; Bonnie Januszewki-Ytuarte and her daughter, Tess, provided terrific and smart ideas, as did Ines Kramer and Elena Greenberg; Dave Hanley read many of these pieces as I was writing them and offered criticism too harsh (especially for a former student) but too useful and insightful to ignore; Nancy Lager and Tim Taylor have always provided a sense of home, a bottle of champagne, and the best conversation in the world; Lewis Burke Frumkes always gets the joke; Fleur and Jerry Laurence laugh at the right places; Liz Hart listened, cheered, and provided a light; Roxanne Coady told me everything I needed to hear about the titles and chapters; Mary Casey Jacob keeps me grounded; Marlana Lytehaause helped me lift off the ground a little and accept my fascination for woo-woo; and Heidi Rockefeller kept my fingers on the keyboard as she kept house around me.

And my family? They get some credit, especially since half the stories are about them. My brother Hugo Barreca remembers the good bits; both he and my niece, Laura—who read early versions of many of these and let me know when I got it right—keep me in line. My stepsons Tim and Matthew Meyer keep me honest and keep me laughing. My sister-in-law, Pat Sherlock, keeps reminding me that I'm not the only one who thinks the way I do.

Finally, the real Bedford/St. Martin's author, my husband, Michael Meyer, not only makes me wonder how I ever got this lucky, but also keeps me eager (not anxious) to see what absurdities and delights each day will bring. No kidding. We fall asleep laughing and wake up laughing. It doesn't get better than this.

IT'S NOT THAT
I'M BITTER...

1

INTRODUCTION TO MY GIRLISH WAY

OF LOOKING AT THINGS

The world lies to us.

Men don't believe the lies. They know it's a load of advertising, a bunch of hype, a song-and-dance number for the easily charmed.

But women believe. We're like those weirdly inarticulate but enthusiastic UFO sighters who live in unpopulated desert towns: we know it's out there, whatever it is.

We're eager to believe it's all possible.

We want to believe it is possible to erase the appearance of fine lines around our delicate eye area with the application of a product made from placenta extract. (We don't want to know whose placenta, however, or be given details concerning how it was extracted: "*Hey*! I wasn't *done* with that yet!")

We want to believe that if we wear a pair of palazzo pants with a latex escape hatch built into the stomach area, we'll appear five pounds slimmer instantly.

We want to believe that highlighting our hair will make us look as if we've been in the sun instead of in a salon with enough chewing-gum-sized pieces of Reynolds Wrap sticking out of our heads to pick up Radio Nepal. On a clear day.

We are eager to believe that soft contact lenses, foam inserts, gel nails, and underwire bras will transform us into soignée creatures so startlingly different from our usual lumpy selves that chance encounters with former college rivals will have them gasping "Is that really *you*?!"

We insist on believing that a flat tummy, toned arms, thin thighs, and a firm neck will make us feel better about ourselves when all it actually takes to feel better is a martini and plate of cheese snacks.

After all, once we hit forty, women have only about four taste buds left: one for vodka, one for wine, one for cheese, and one for chocolate. Beyond a certain point, flat, toned, thin, and firm are all things best left to those for whom they are negotiable assets. Those of us with sufficient assets have earned the right to sit on them and be comfortable.

And yet we torture ourselves, even though we are smart broads.

We know better than to believe in our heart of hearts that applying "minerals" to our faces will actually reduce the apparent size of our pores. We know that the use of finely ground rocks to act as sealant is best referred to as "grouting" and should be done by a licensed contractor and not by a teenager at Sephora whose pores are microscopic. Yet we buy the whole face-grouting kit so that we can get a "free" cosmetic bag. The cosmetic bag will remain unused and, eventually, we will give it to a niece or Goodwill.

Deep down, most of us realize that to "behave youthfully" will not make us seem like Demi Moore or Susan Sarandon, and will most certainly not net us Ashton Kutcher or Tim Robbins, but will instead prompt others to consider us as either Mrs. Robinson from *The Graduate* (if they are our good friends) or as Bette Davis from *What Ever Happened to Baby Jane?* (if they are everyone else). More about this later.

We torture ourselves by wondering if we are too old for headbands.

We spend time pondering the judicious use of bangs.

When an attractive man (or, for that matter, a woman—who has time to be picky?) has flashed a dazzling smile in our direction without provocation, we spend the afternoon wondering if they noticed the insouciant way our bag and shoes create a stylistic dialectic, or noticed the whimsical yet edgy use of our accessories.

We like watchbands, bracelets, and interesting buttons. We are women who believe that what we need is a makeover and stylist when we fear that what we really need is a sandblaster, caps, and our stomachs stapled.

And yet, I repeat, we are smart broads. Really.

We are the feminists who still care what we look like at the beach and care deeply about the bathing suits we buy.

Let me tell you about swimwear. Let me tell you, specifically, about bathing-suit season at T.J. Maxx.

There I was, in April. I knew it was a low self-esteem day because I went to try on bathing suits while wearing knee-high socks. My legs haven't seen the sun in nine months, I'm the color of a flounder, and there I am, wearing cable-knit, pine green, slightly restrictive knee-high socks.

(Men have no idea what this means. No man—no straight man in Western civilization, that is—has ever tried on a bathing suit. Men wear the bathing suit their mothers bought them when they were seventeen until there's a hole where they put their keys, and then they walk into some cheap store, find the sale bin, find a suit, hold it up, say, "It's blue; it'll fit," and then they leave.)

Women, as I said, torture ourselves. I'm not the only one. It's a rainy day, maybe fifty degrees, as far from summer as imaginable, and yet there are all these other women around my age. Pretty much everybody is my age; my age is most easily defined as too old for work-study, too young for cremation. We're huddled behind the cheap curtains at T.J. Maxx. We have all brought in our seven garments. We are isolated in front of the unforgiving mirrors under fluorescent lights that give us the flattering contours of pot cheese, and I'm hearing these noises of the kind made by victims of the Spanish Inquisition: "owhhh," "arghhh," and "nwwwwccchhh."

And I have my seven pieces, too, don't forget, all of which look ridiculous even on the hanger. You know how recently the big thing was "draw the eye upward"? There are bells and feathers and buttons and spangles everywhere around the neckline. I'm looking for a bathing suit with a live ferret on the shoulder, since that is the one thing guaranteed to "draw the eye upward."

And why is it that the fashion fascists tell us to "draw the eye upward" anyway? Because they can't say, "You don't want them to look at your fat ass, do you?" That's why. Because we all know that's what "draw the eye upward" actually means.

But one question occurs to me in a flash of insight, in a flash of inspiration: "Who's looking at women my age at the beach?"

Let's face it: everybody's looking at beautiful eighteen-year-olds. They're like gazelles; it's like watching them in their native habitat on one of those *Planet Earth* programs. They're chasing Frisbees, volleyballs, Hacky Sacks, and playing in the wide-open spaces like Labrador puppies.

Can we tell the truth here? Not that I'm bitter, but the only people looking at fifty-year-old women on the beach are other fifty-year-old women, every single one of whom is elbowing whatever poor soul she's sitting next to and saying, "Do I look like her? No, come on, do I look like her? Look, that one there, the big one, do I look like . . . ?" And then there's the million-dollar question: "Be honest. Do I look like her *from the back?*"

So as I was trying on this off-the-shoulder "Jones of New York" with ruffles and polka dots, I thought, *Gina, if you bought this suit and wore it to the beach, you could make three hundred women happy instantly, profoundly, enduringly. Because they would all look at themselves and then look at you and go, "I might not look too good, but I don't look like her."*

I didn't buy it. I bought a one-piece black number that was as close to a burka as I could find. So much for sisterhood.

You have to admit that life is a riot once you start paying attention.

And I worry about the next generation of young women, too.

A few years ago I was telling my class at the University of Connecticut a story about growing up in the sixties and seventies and listening to such high-self-esteem songs as "Love Has No Pride" and "Tell Him." "Tell Him" includes possibly the worst advice ever given to women—repeatedly telling a man that you love him will not bond you more closely to his soul but will instead cause him to join the Witness Protection Program. He will change his identity and move to one those states where they wear Dacron and see UFOs. Remember "I Will Follow Him." That was another doozy. My students are attentive (after all, I grade them), but at one point a young woman in the back of the room raised her hand and pointed out that "two full generations have passed since you were growing up, Professor." I thanked her for sharing and then told her, gently, that she had failed the class.

But I decided to go and listen to some new music. That week it so happened that the cover of *Time* magazine pictured a singer-songwriter named Jewel. Her hit song was called "You Were Meant for Me." I don't know whether it's actually been named the theme song for clinical depression, but I think it should be. It goes something like: "I get up in the morning and you're not here, even though you were meant for me. I make one egg, but I don't clean the pan. I go to the movies, but I leave early because you were meant for me. I go home, I cook the other egg in the dirty pan because you were meant for me," et cetera.

What? We've only come this far? This is what's happened after forty years of the women's movement.

At least with "I Will Follow Him," we got off our asses.

Not that I'm bitter.

Yet these are young women who pay their own bills, write their own papers, and fight their own ideological battles. They bring home the bacon, fry it up in the pan, et cetera. They want a boyfriend, sure, but mostly for the weekend—Monday through Friday, they are busy revising the rules, not bending to them.

Speaking of the rules: In 1996, I appeared on Oprah debating with two "girls" who had written a book titled *The Rules* (I call them girls because that's what they called themselves. They are exactly my age. We all graduated from high school in 1975 and even if women are still, at least according to the ex-president of Harvard, deficient in math skills, every woman can figure out how old another woman is. We can also figure out each other's weight as if we were running a booth at a state fair.) So we all came of age at the same time. They also grew up hearing "I Will Follow Him."

I expected to find a common ground; instead, I found pay dirt. On Oprah's stage I faced a blonde and a brunette; the brunette did not speak. And I don't want to sound nasty, but the blonde was as blond as I am. Let's just say I don't think the drapes and the rug matched. We argued on television like a bunch of women from the Bronx yelling at each other through tenement windows and over clotheslines. They wanted to know, as the blonde put it, "why you have such a problem with our book, Dr. Barreca." (She made the word "Dr." sound like "bloodsucking leech.") I replied, "I have a problem with your book because it assumes that men are morons and that women are capable of infinite manipulation; you tell women that the only way to get a man to marry them is to withhold sex as long as possible. You say, 'Never laugh out loud in front of a man. Save the laughter for your girlfriends.' And: 'No matter how hot the sex gets, you must remain cool.' What I want to know is, if you can't laugh out loud, and you can't have hot sex, why on earth would you want a husband?"

Why, in other words, should any of us do battle with these stereotypes? Why not just become one of the *Rules* girls? If we believed what they told us, we wouldn't have to get our hands dirty and we'd never be late for work. Oh, right, we probably wouldn't be going out to work, either.

Hmmm. . . .

Oh, right: because it doesn't work. As a *People* magazine article from 2001 by Alex Tresniowski put it in "There Goes the Bride," "Nothing in Ellen Fein's Rules Seems to Apply to Her Bitter Divorce." I actually received several calls from magazines and newspapers around the country when the story of this divorce broke—I'm quoted in the *People* piece—because reporters wanted to know how I felt about Fein's divorce.

"As a feminist," I replied, "I am always saddened to hear when a woman's professional life is undermined by matters from her personal life. And as soon as I stop laughing my ass off, I'll be happy to explain this dynamic in more detail."

Let's face it: when you cave, you are buying, however subtly, into the idea that it is easier to please the master than to learn mastery—that you are getting what you need by the privilege of your sex rather than by the right of your humanity. You have to be nice to the guy who pumps your gas, checks your oil, or buys you a house and pays your bills. That whole "bending and breaking and

remaking the rules"? That's, *pffft,* out the window; you can't afford that luxury anymore.

He's "providing" for you because he's happy with your company.
If he becomes unhappy with you, or if the placenta stuff around
your eyes gives birth to new wrinkles and that tummy panel finally
blows so that you inflate like a pontoon, he has every right to kick
you out of his house and refuse to pay your bills. You are there not
by right but by privilege.

Of course, that might just be my girlish way of looking at
things. . . .

My role is to notice patterns of foolishness in our collective human behavior and to chronicle them. It turns out that, except for
the *Rules* girls, we're all pretty much alike. We all believe we're too
bitchy, too judgmental, too jealous, too loud, too easy, too much,
too crazy, too messy, too greedy, too passive. Some of these I would
like to change, but mostly I just want to look at them. Mostly I just
want to point and laugh.

Let's examine what else we've been told all these years, shall
we? Let's cast our gaze outward rather than upward.

Don't be distracted by the ferret.

2

AM I TURNING INTO ONE OF

THE SMITH BROTHERS?

You spend about fifteen minutes in front of the mirror every morning trying to see yourself in a new light.

To be more precise, you are trying to see your chin in a new light.

Armed with tweezers, reading glasses, and a mirror, you are a woman on a mission.

Once you begin, you are unstoppable. You have the kind of concentration envied by army generals and nuclear physicists. Nothing can distract you or dissuade you from the absolute necessity of your pursuit. Small children can scream, alarms can wail, windows can shatter, the earth itself can move beneath your feet, but you cannot, will not, look away.

You will get that rogue hair. The one you can only see from a certain angle in a certain light. The one so fiercely connected to your person that it must be part of your skeletal structure. You will pull it and triumph. In so doing you will feel a mixture of vindication and exultation both, a sense of victory almost unparalleled. Holding the hair up to look at it more carefully is like ridiculing a vanquished foe.

It is like winning a fabulous prize. It is an accomplishment, a final thwarting of an enemy, a valedictory.

Except, of course, that women are not supposed to have chin hairs. This means that a person, however bold in alternate venues, would collapse instantly if somebody caught her in the act of plucking. Imagine her guy walking in and saying, "Hello, sweetheart! Gee, what are you doing?" The woman would have to say, "I'm trying to do my own root canal. That's the only reason I had my lower jaw stuck out this way," and she'd start tugging on her molar with the tweezers to make the whole pantomime look real.

Life, as you know, is not fair. Some men have backs so hairy it looks like they're always wearing angora sweaters. Yet a couple of little white hairs and suddenly a woman feels like she should be auditioning for the opening scene of Macbeth. Like Blanche DuBois, she's afraid to be seen under a naked lightbulb even if the guy looking at her is Karl Malden.

So while, historically, women hid behind fans and veils, we now cup our chins in meetings and keep our faces pointed downward in what might appear to be an attempt at flirtation but what is really an attempt not to attract glare. See how many women you can catch staring at their chins in the rearview mirror when stopped at a light.

There's always one hair you can only see when you're in the car. I've seen women trying to use the Velcro from the back of their E-ZPass to remove that one. You have to get it while you're in the vehicle itself. You can never see it anywhere else. But once in the car, it looks like you've been grooming it for years, nurturing it along so that it's grown luxuriantly and with gusto, like you've been feeding it fertilizer and intend to do a comb-over with it.

Women live in fear that everybody else has been looking at that hair for years while they've been oblivious, going along, lalala, concerned one day about the size of their ankles and the next about the size of their bank account, when all they should have been obsessing over was the Hair That Could Strangle Pittsburgh.

In contrast, there are ads during prime-time network television for men's razors; there are devices, for goodness' sake, just to get the hair out of men's noses and ears. Can you imagine if women had vast quantities of hair growing in our noses and ears? Men would be shrieking and waving their hands in the air, running away as if from werewolves.

Men would not, for example, buy women little nose-hair clippers on our birthdays. They would not say with a little affectionate laugh, "Hon, do you think maybe you should trim your ears before we take the family photograph?"

If women had tufts growing from our noses and ears, men would bring exorcists to the house. They would hire professionals to drive the evil spirits from our bodies. And the ones doing it would be seen as optimists, because most men would move away and keep the shades down lest a hirsute babe walk by without warning.

But the time has come to admit this much out loud: I've got a couple of lousy, almost invisible hairs on my face. And I want them to stop making me nuts.

For years I hid my tweezers the way alcoholics conceal bottles, stashing them in the top drawers of ornamental cabinets and hiding them inside bags so that nobody could unwittingly stumble across them and know what they hide. I mean, you might have one cheap pair for your eyebrows, but when you get out the Swiss-crafted stainless steel, everybody knows what's going on; you can't hide from the unsightly hair police.

In my house, every mirror has a pair near it. Every pocketbook. Every suitcase, too, despite my worry that a TSA security agent will one day shout to a fellow officer, "Hey, Ralphie, are the *Leatherman Irongrip Tweezers in this here lady's luggage* permitted on the flight?" "What is she, Wolfman Jack's sister?" That scene would be followed by outright prolonged laughter from the other 3,437 fellow passengers gathered around me. Including George Clooney.

Magnifying mirrors—starting at 3x and going up to 10x—have proved harder to hide. But I have lots of these as well, having developed a particular fondness for the ones with sticky-adhesive cups on the back so you can attach them like reflective starfish to any shiny surface. I stare into them as if gazing into a crystal ball.

Ah, self-reflection: if only it ended with the chin. But life is not so easy. . . .

Have you ever looked into one of those magnifying mirrors and discovered your pores are so huge that your face looks like something from the lunar landscape? Or perhaps you have, as I do in my office, a full-length mirror that makes you look four inches shorter and twenty pounds heavier than you actually are?

Do you spend time scanning your face and your body the way a proofreader scans a legal document? Do you have days when you think your looks are pretty good and other days when you think it would just be easier to put a bag over your head and a tent over your body before you leave the house? Does it matter when people tell you that they perceive no difference whatsoever between how you look on one of your really "good" days and how you look on one of your really "terrible" days? When they say such things, do you want to smack them?

Have you ever said to anyone, "Does this barrette make my head look fat?"

If you answered "yes" to any of these questions, my bet is that you're a girly woman; this particular brand of self-torture is supremely girly behavior. I wouldn't call it womanly because I reserve the word "womanly" for the more mature, practical activities I associate with being an adult. When I'm driven to distraction by the fact that I've only just noticed that my eyebrows seem crooked, however, I'm just living life as a girl.

It doesn't change much with age, either. I'm getting puppet lines around my mouth like a ventriloquist's dummy; that's new; that's glorious. And also, after a few hours, no matter what brand I use, my lipstick now starts to feather. That's the word they use—"feather"—but what is really happening is that my mouth seems to be seeping or spreading into the rest of my face like a stain. I've turned into one big advertisement for industrial-strength lip liner. Terribly attractive.

As far as I can tell, men don't do this to themselves. They look at themselves once in the morning and maybe they check their hair and their teeth toward the end of the day, before drinks and dinner, to make sure no food has lodged in either over the course of the afternoon. But they do not obsess the way we do. My husband, for example, is decidedly unsympathetic when I whine after looking into my 10x mirror for twenty minutes after having noticed yet another crease around my mouth or line in my forehead.

"Why do you do that to yourself?" he asks me.

For him this is not a rhetorical question.

"How can you not do this to yourself?" I reply. "Don't you want to see the slow erosion of that which you once laughingly referred to as 'your looks'? Aren't you interested in cataloging every flaw, blemish, and splotch?"

In all innocence, he asks, "Why on earth would anybody do that?"

I usually laugh and say it's the inherited behavior pattern, something genetically encoded, for the female of the species, rather like an appreciation of dollhouse miniatures or shoes with sparkles on them. He's stopped listening by this point, so it's always fine.

This morning, however, when I did my usual "I look awful today," checking out my potential back fat by looking over my shoulder, after having just put on a favorite suit, he said, "But I've always liked you in that outfit."

"But today I look like I bought it for somebody else. I refuse to be appeased."

He kept watching me as I examined myself. It was as if we were two observers looking at a third person. "You don't look any different from how you looked this weekend," he pointed out. "You didn't instantly assume gargantuan proportions or inflate like a life raft in the last forty-eight hours."

"But I looked better on Saturday!"

"You know what? I don't know how to break this to you, but you looked exactly the same. Same haircut, same face, same body."

"But somehow the combination looks all wrong right now."

"I'm telling you, you look exactly the same. Maybe you just don't feel as good. But don't blame the suit."

I can reel off all the reasons I do this to myself starting from when Doctor held me up and said, "Mrs. Barreca, you have a cute baby girl." (When my brother was born, apparently the doctor said, "You have a big, strong baby boy.")

I can tell you from an anthropological, sociological, biological, psychological (and economic! let's not forget economic) reason why I've inherited this script. And I can also tell you, in alphabetical order, a hundred reasons why this self-destructive behavior is worse than useless, not only for me but pretty much for every woman who feels this way.

Feminist, schmeminist. I want to look better than I look.

For example, I've just reached the age where I'm scared of hotel mirrors, of those unfamiliar and disinterested reflections. I'm nervous when I see myself out of context. Hotel mirrors give me new perspectives and that's no longer what I'm looking for. I want to see the version of myself that I know. Lit from the side and seen from two angles simultaneously, I can no longer tell myself that a man half my age would find me attractive. If I could just see myself straight-on with my carefully rehearsed and prepared spontaneous smile, in good lighting, it does seem at least possible. But seeing with no filters, with no familiarity, my rounded shoulders, my soft upper arms, the way the backs of my legs look, then all pretense falls away. Home is not only where the heart is; it's also where the good mirrors are.

The trouble is, all this knowledge gets eclipsed by the image in the mirror, the image that doesn't give me back what I hope to see. I can eat light or, worse, eat "lite," wear good clothes, and buy reasonable, non-clown cosmetics, and I can take care of myself.

But gradually, my longing to improve my looks via The Body Shop is being replaced by a longing to improve my looks via Photoshop. It's far easier and so much less messy, after all.

When I consider what it will be like when my "lite" is spent, when I think about facing issues far graver than whether my mascara is clumping, I want to do better, not just look better. I want to have less disdain and contempt for my body—this encasement that's held up pretty well so far.

I want to remind myself that I shouldn't worry so much about how my body looks as be grateful for the fact that most of it works. When I meet my own eyes in a reflection, I'd like to see the wisdom in them rather than the bags under them. When I glance at my legs, I want to remember the places they've taken me rather than how they looked when I was seventeen. And I want to remind myself that objects in the mirror are cuter than they appear.

3

DON'T SAY "COUGAR"

LIKE IT'S A BAD THING

Do you know how old Anne Bancroft was when she played Mrs. Robinson, the quintessential older woman, in the 1967 movie *The Graduate*? Thirty-six. Let me repeat that: *Anne Bancroft* was *thirty-six years old* when she played Mrs. Robinson.

I take it personally.

Think about it: Dustin Hoffman himself was thirty when he played the role of a twenty-one-year-old. No surprise there, since male actors are apparently ageless. In contrast, Bancroft, all of six years older than her male co-star, played Mrs. Robinson, who was supposed to be forty—old enough to be his mother.

Mrs. Robinson was the original cougar.

You know what a cougar is, right? She is a woman between forty and sixty who pursues men in their twenties or thirties sexually.

Obviously she's pursuing them sexually. What else would you pursue them for? It's not for conversation, and it's certainly not for fashion advice. It's not because once you're perimenopausal you have a sudden urge to start playing Frisbee golf or beer pong.

And God knows their lines of credit are even shorter than their attention spans.

But in 1967, Mrs. Robinson's crush on a guy nineteen years her junior nevertheless defined her so clearly as a deviant, as someone on the scary side of a woman's life, as a person obviously just one step away from the grave, as a woman so nearly about to trade her patent-leather stilettos for a stainless-steel walker, that she scared several generations of women away from admitting that young men were, for lack of a better word, adorable. The movie implied that no normal woman would feel like Mrs. Robinson.

Now we know better.

Everybody likes young people. Why does this come as a shock? Of course Mrs. Robinson could be attracted to her daughter's suitor; the only inexplicable part of the plot was that Mrs. Robinson, in her sexy fishnets and fabulous eyeliner, could find a young man as extremely nerdy and useless as Benjamin (aka "scuba gear boy") attractive. *That* is the only aspect of the film that is now perplexing to the average cinemaphile.

Mrs. Robinson, unlike her contemporary counterpart Samantha, played by Kim Cattrall in *Sex in the City,* is portrayed as vaguely pathetic even though she is whoppingly attractive—the original and definitive MILF.

Yet it's her daughter the graduate Benjamin wants, not Mrs. Robinson herself, never mind that the daughter has the glassy-eyed stare of the congenitally vapid, not to mention being as sophisticated as, say, suet.

Mrs. Robinson is at the mercy of her world because she's stuck in a conventional life, whereas Samantha in *SITC* shows the world no mercy and in fact brings it to heel.

But it's somehow still newsworthy that a woman past forty could like a man under forty. In contrast, of course, every fifteen minutes a study comes out proving that the reason older men are drawn to younger women is because of a universal, inexorable genetic predisposition for choosing the mates who will be able to bear their seed to fruition.

I suspect that the reason all these scientific studies prove that old men need to hook up with younger women is because the studies are funded by those who might best be described as "old men," being in control as they are of major foundations, if not of their own bodily functions.

(Their conversations go something like this: "Sorry, honey, I need to begin life anew with Fawn [or Mysti, Bambi, or Raine, or all three if part of a religious cult] because my DNA insists that I bed down with a neurasthenic, long-legged nymphette with a Brazilian wax who's been on the pill since she was thirteen, eats only kiwis and egg whites, and who's going to clearly be the one to mother my next litter of children. Kiss the grandkids for me!")

As far as I can tell, and I've looked, huge pharmaceutical companies are not awarding grants for major research institutions to justify—oh, I'm sorry, to *illuminate*—the scientific underpinnings of why older women also like younger men. In part that's because it's always been a secret, one of those just-us-girls pieces of information.

One thing we have to unlearn is that we're not the evil witch out of "Hansel and Gretel," inviting the orphan of the forest into the oven to be baked and served up for lunch when we're attracted to someone younger than ourselves. It doesn't mean that we're Blanche DuBois and going after someone who's more or less paperboy age.

And if you think it's bad that Mrs. Robinson is forty, just consider the fact that Blanche DuBois from *A Streetcar Named Desire,* a character who has to put a paper lantern over the lightbulb so that she can disguise her age from a potential suitor, is all of thirty-four years old.

Think about just how old a man has to be in order to be cast as an Older Man by Hollywood: he has to be on the way to his cremation for this to occur. And even then he'll get a cute nurse.

Life mimics art here: I've been watching the news closely, and I haven't seen any limpid-eyed young men following Nancy Pelosi around. Apparently, the use of power as an aphrodisiac is gender specific; presumably, tough cookies don't crumble at the touch of a sweet young thing with great abs.

Not that I'm bitter. Because, as we all know, there are now plenty of older women married to younger men.

Let's think of some older women–younger men couples: we've got Demi Moore and Ashton Kutcher, plus there's Susan Sarandon and Tim Robbins.

That's it.

Men don't age. That's the problem. Remember the classic line from *All About Eve*? Margo Channing, played by Bette Davis at her most bête noir, says of her talented and charming playwright paramour, "Bill's thirty-two. He looks thirty-two. He looked it five years ago; he'll look it twenty years from now. I hate men."

Margo herself, in contrast, is "not twenty-ish, I'm not thirty-ish. Three months ago I was forty years old. Forty. Four O. That slipped out. I hadn't quite made up my mind to admit it. Now I suddenly feel as if I've taken all my clothes off."

Nothing is fair. Tony Randall could have a baby, Larry King could have a baby, Saul Bellow could have a baby—these were all guys who were born before the Earth's crust cooled, and you can bet that they did not have these kids with any woman whose estrogen level or waistline wasn't perfect. These were guys who became fathers when they were so old they were falling asleep in the Fisher-Price aisle of Toys "R" Us as their nannies shopped for their tots.

Guys keep quoting the Bible to tell us how many kings had children when they were 420 years old, as if they were somehow going to find a passage where the prescription for Viagra was encoded in Deuteronomy.

Part of what puzzles me about the whole age business is that I'm still thinking that I'm not as old as I thought my parents were when they were my age.

Our parents were way, way older at our age than we are, and that's not just wishful thinking or denial. That's a fact, a bona fide genuine difference. One more reference to a classic film—I know, I know, I am showing my age—but do you remember *Marty*?

(Either version—I know, I've written about it elsewhere, but it is a great film.) In *Marty,* the title character's washed-up, washed-out, clawed-hand, saggy-baggy-dress-wearing "old" Italian mother says, "I'm fifty-four years old, I have strength in my hands, I want to cook, I want to clean. . . ."

She was *fifty-four years old.*

I don't think of fifty-four as *old*. But they did.

And they were right, because for them it meant they were of the older generation, that they had fully lived their lives. So there's a legacy about age and fear and the ending of life that we need to shake off, like a dog shaking off rain or mud. This isn't ours, even if we've rolled around in it and are covered with it. We're not as old as they were at the same number.

Now maybe you don't have this same baggage with your family, but my mother died when she was forty-seven. Think about it: forty-seven. That's not enough time to pack; that's the middle of the first half of the second act; that's a walk-on part in life, a cameo appearance. You don't even get your name listed in the credits if your part is that brief.

So maybe all that gave me a kind of rush on time, a sense that I'd better get my act in gear if I'm going to get anything done, leave anything behind me at all, and that's fueled the writing and the speaking and teaching—all of which have accelerated in order to compensate for having no children of my own, a need to make an impression another way, through words, through convincing myself that what I do, every once in a while, can make a difference.

This is no brag; it's a way of figuring out how to justify my life.

And that's part of the business of being a grown-up, I suspect: figuring out what counts for real and not just what you believe "should" count and then using that to keep you doing what you do every day. Sure, there are times I would have wished other things for myself—it would have been fun to be a Rockette, to have learned to juggle, and to have been a train robber—and I still hope for a few secret, *shhhh,* achievements. But there are some things no longer within my reach, and I've made peace with that; I no longer fall asleep hungry for what will never appear on my menu.

Just don't believe anyone, woman or girl, who tells you that she doesn't dream about what's on somebody else's menu every once in a while.

Life is great, but it isn't easy.

Now let's talk about one of the reasons it isn't easy: facing the larger issues raised when a very young woman attaches herself romantically to an older man in a position of power.

Let's define "very young women" as those barely at a legal drinking age. (It's tough to drink Dom Perignon when the woman you're taking out to dinner still orders a Diet Dr Pepper, so most of these babes have legal ID.) These are not the ones who still order Happy Meals on a regular basis. But if her dad is closer in age to the guy she pursues than she is, and if her mom has to be called in for questioning at the Vice Principal's (or the Special Prosecutor's) request in order to answer questions about her child's behaviors and whereabouts, then she is very young.

She's young enough to want to Sleep with the Boss but not old enough to want to Be the Boss. She wants to handle and manipulate power but not to possess it herself; she particularly wants others to notice that she can enthrall and entice without bothering with all usual ordinary and everyday niceties of having to earn a position of authority.

She likes to sit in the lap of Authority and play with Authority's mustache.

What is she (this quintessential girly character) going after when she goes after the idolized older man?

I say it's pride, rather than lust, motivating her. I know for a fact that she's not talking herself into this, either; she really feels the longing to be on this older guy's arm, sitting on his lap, lying across his bed. The boss—genuinely, sincerely, absolutely—appeals to the young woman. The girly girl sighs, pouts, and swoons over the idea of him, even when he looks like Yoda. Or, heaven help us, Donald Trump.

Why?

I feel confident about discussing the allure of the boss because I've been that girly girl. I'm not her anymore, however, and these days for me to develop a crush on a *much* older man would involve learning how to use techniques of flirtation most often witnessed on the TV program *ER* when the entire team is yelling, "Clear!"

But in my day I've had crushes on pretty much every guy I looked up to, worked for, or whose class I attended. There was no common denominator between them except for the fact that they all ran the show.

So it's not that I don't like older and powerful men. Some are sort of cute. Even the ones who aren't cute often exude an intriguing mix of power, charm, and savoir faire (French for "lots o' money"), all of which makes them attractive to the typical young woman. Such guys might especially appeal to a significantly younger woman within their circle of influence even when their allure is starting to fade among those ladies who have known them longer, better, or before they joined the Hair Club for Men. Or the "Viagra Users Consciousness-Raising Group" for that matter.

The young woman in their thrall, however, swears that from a certain angle the boss looks like Liam Neeson, Daniel Day-Lewis, Josh Hartnett, or any other alpha male who can act the chin-clenching-but-secretly-vulnerable role to perfection.

This happens to almost every woman at some point in her life: She falls for an inappropriate man. She makes him the center of her attention and desires, and she becomes oblivious to his disinterest. I remember telling a friend that I was relieved to find my therapist unattractive; I described him as a bulky man with thin lips. "Yeah," she said. "Give it three months and you'll be talking about how terribly adorable his thin lips are."

But most women can recognize, after a certain point in the fantasy, that these relationships will not necessarily yield the real-life romance they're looking for. In most cases, the woman will then turn her affections to more realistic visions: the man sitting next to her at a lecture, the friend working beside her in the office, a gentleman who will listen to her without billing Blue Cross.

I'm not the only one making this gross generalization. Remember the wonderful midlife crisis movie *City Slickers*? At one point Billy Crystal explains the whole situation very clearly: "Women need a reason to have sex. Men just need a place." And we all remember his other great line, where he suggests that a friend start examining his relationship preferences: "Have you noticed that the older you get, the younger your girlfriends get?" Crystal's character says, "Pretty soon you'll be dating sperm."

Let's face it: some (perhaps not all, but certainly some) fellows regard attempted seduction of any new female in their territory as a sort of extracurricular service, regarding it as both their right and their duty. And I'm not male-bashing here, or even engaging in the kind of sexual elitism as egregious and damaging as that perpetrated by the worst of the bad old system. Trust me, I am thrilled to believe that things change for the better and that the men who accept positions of authority are respectful in all ways of those younger and more vulnerable than themselves.

I also fully believe—because I have seen it—that male mentors and bosses can encourage, inspire, nurture, and support the women in their midst without ever casting a shadow of inappropriate sexuality, and that the increasing number of women leaders can do the same with the young men who pass through their offices.

But I also believe that if young women fall for the powerful man, there are also powerful men who will fall for the young woman. I know men who believe that a ripe female employee of their very own is one of the perquisites of the job, something between a company car and a really terrific dental plan. I know otherwise quite decent men who lurk near the desks of women whose livelihoods depend in part on following the whims and orders of their bosses, who might feel as if they have to look interested in order to keep their jobs. (This scenario should remind us of Judy Holliday's classic response to a director who was chasing her around a casting couch: at one point she stopped, removed the falsies she was wearing, and—handing two spheres of foam rubber to her pursuer—said, "I believe it's these you're after.")

These men's seductions most accurately translate into the following: "I'm attracted to you sexually and would like to begin a relationship. But you must understand that our affair—and make no mistake about it, it will be an affair and not the beginning of a primary relationship—will have to remain clandestine, be short-termed, and run completely according to my schedule. Okay?"

As far as I can tell, this sums up the first season of *Mad Men*.

But if our culture encourages young women to go after powerful men, it equally suggests that powerful men have every right to go after young women. A friend of mine was recently claiming a morally righteous stance when I questioned him concerning his predilection for dating women much younger than himself. He brought up the award-winning film with Jack Nicholson *As Good As It Gets,* wherein Nicholson is beloved by the much younger star, Helen Hunt.

Citing the undeniable nature of this cinematic evidence for the sound nature of my friend's position, I nevertheless suggested that he repeat to himself the following: "I am not Jack, what I saw was a fictional movie, and I should not believe that It Gets That Good for Me."

Finally, what is *most* curious about the attraction between publicly powerful men and younger, less powerful women is that, for both, the object of desire is pretty much indistinguishable from any other object occupying the same position. We laugh at the stories circulating about what went on in the White House a couple of administrations ago because, larger political implications aside, it is *silly* to think about two people playing spin the bottle in the Oval Office. An intern is an intern is an intern, and a President is, well, just a President, not a specific person to love— except for those who loved him before he knew where he'd be working.

The fun part about real relationships is, after all, the knowledge that you are loved and admired for who you are, not for what you do or how you look or because you showed up at the right place when somebody was feeling amorous. This is what should make us genuinely proud: the thought that we can, despite the odds, despite all the false allurements out there, construct a meaning-ful relationship with somebody we actually know. Simple? Yes. Easy? No.

That's why it is an accomplishment.

4

WHO IS YOUR KING CHARMING?

Can there even be such a creature as "King Charming"?

Prince Charming we know. He's a polygamist, the main figure of one of those cults where there are 758 kids and women all
have the unibrow and wear *Little House on the Prairie* throwback
dresses. Prince Charming marries Snow White, Cinderella, Sleeping Beauty, and for all we know he's also knocked up Mother
Goose. Who knows? Maybe he's also responsible for all those kids
who live in a shoe.

(You know the real rhyme, right? "There was an old woman
who lived in a shoe / She had so many children, she didn't know
what to do / Try as she would, she could not detect / which was
the cause, and which the effect.")

Prince Charming is just a reprobate, what the Brits would call "a lad" and what delusional women all over America would refer to as a "hot guy with commitment issues."

What I want to know is this: what happens to Prince Charming after forty?

How come he never becomes King Charming?

Is it because once a man becomes King, he doesn't need to charm anymore? Is it because once he's got the throne, scepter, crown—or the corner office, the Lexus, and the hair plugs—he simply bosses everybody around, charm be damned, and since no one can afford to say the Emperor's not wearing clothes (or point out that the clothes he's wearing are badly tailored, the wrong palate for his preternaturally pale skin, and generally ill conceived for someone of his age) he lives in blissful unawareness of the small pleasures he awards to those who have the rather scanty reciprocal privilege of serving at his pleasure?

Not that I'm bitter.

The man who would be King is not a man who needs to charm; the man who would be King insists on being charmed.

What would King Charming look like and act like, were such a creature to exist?

As I'm writing, I'm sitting with my young friend Sarah (whom I accused of being twenty-nine and who instantly corrected me; she's twenty-eight) and my old friend Dozer—and when I say "old" I mean "long-term." We are three smart women of different backgrounds, perspectives, and tastes in men, all involved in what are conventionally known as "happy relationships," depending on the hour, the state of the economy, and where we are in our hormonal cycles.

We're discussing possible models for King Charming as seriously as the attendees at the G 8 Summit discuss Climate Investment Funds. We ask: would King Charming necessarily be better than Prince Charming? We ask: is Prince Charming just a poorly Xeroxed copy of the King?

Dozer asks whether King Charming would be all shriveled up and gnarled, wizard-like, resembling Steve Tyler and Mick Jagger? "Perhaps," Sarah chimes in, "King Charming would be pontoonlike, mirroring Elvis in his white-spangled-suit phase or John Travolta in *Primary Colors.*

The words "King" and "Charming" don't even go together. But maybe they will once this new crop of Royals takes over. Apparently our choice of Charmings, however, depends quite a bit on our sexual preference.

A devoted and fabulous friend in New York who loves Barbra Streisand movies, Paul Stuart suits, *Vogue, All About Eve,* Paris during Fashion Week, fine literature, brilliant humor, and just happens—oh, *quelle* surprise!—to be a gay man recently sent me a news item that has entirely captured my imagination: "A gay dating Web site has submitted the results of an interesting poll. Over a third of gay men have expressed romantic interest in Prince Harry, only 23 percent prefer William, and a good third of the polled population would steer clear of either."

The snippet (I refer to the bit from the paper, not my friend, although "The Snippet" would be a great nickname for somebody who routinely fed one excellent small pieces of delicious gossip) went on to explain that "the poll expressed hope that people like Harry and William, constrained by their exclusive monarchy, would be pleased to learn that they could arouse such strong emotions in their homosexual subjects."

Naturally, that makes collecting this delicious gossip perfectly okay. As long as strong emotions are aroused in a purely disinterested manner—with research carried out in support of the monarchy and not for any prurient reasons, like figuring out who would be more fun in bed or have a better profile, Speedo-wise—then we can all get behind the findings. So to speak.

Far less interesting to me, I'll admit, was that the Web site "also polled lesbians to learn more about their preferences: 23 percent picked William's girlfriend Kate Middleton while 18 percent opted for Harry's girl Chelsy Davy." It's not that I am uninterested in beautiful women—of course I am, if only as a way to flagellate myself by comparing myself to the impossibly gorgeous and the impossibly young—but I have no idea who these girls are; even though I deliberately choose the longest line at Stop & Shop in order to read as much of the *National Enquirer* as possible, I couldn't identify Chelsy Davy if she were ringing up my Raisin Bran.

I initiated an immediate nonscientific survey that confirmed the Harry-versus-William poll's findings. I did this by calling my girlfriends. In a way that the future King of England would no doubt find extremely depressing, it became clear that the middle-aged women of America think William is adorable. Research indicated that if one calls my girlfriends late on a Friday evening after they've had a few glasses of wine, one discovers that they will also admit to wishing they could be more than one of William's mere erstwhile colonial subjects. "Forget closing your eyes and thinking of England," said Jan. "I'd keep mine wide open and think about how the sun never sets on the British Empire. Let's just say he's a vigorous young man and one expects a great deal from the throne." "He's got that killer smile, just like Diana," sighed Karen. "And that's the only problem I could really imagine: it would remind me too much about his mother and I might get all weepy and not enjoy the sex enough. Although I probably could work my way through that in about three seconds."

William was cooed at and referred to as "compassionate," "determined," "alpha-male in all the fun ways," and "wise." Personally I balk at "wise"; a boy is a boy is a boy. But I do like the smile, the thatch of thick hay-colored hair, the lanky ease he displays on the polo field, his obvious sense of connectedness to the disadvantaged. His noble mien and his ability to withstand the glare of public scrutiny, combined with an instinctive charm and extraordinarily good teeth (not something I associate with the English, and I lived there for five years), make him Special. King material.

What we all deserve, in other words.

Harry, in contrast, is whom a lot of us got. The one who makes trouble. The one who insists that the party keep going even when everyone else wants to go home. The one who acts out. The one who will make us wince when we're with our really fancy friends. He raises no such affections, accolades, and uninhibited approval from the group I polled. "The guy wore a Nazi uniform to a Halloween party, for chrissake; even as the second-in-line to the kingdom, he has no class," is how Jan summed it up. "He has no sense of decorum. He probably really likes Paris Hilton; William no doubt simply tolerates her company," is how Karen put it.

Most women want to spank Harry and not in a fun way. He's really too much of a boy for us to find him intriguing. He seems bratty; he appears unappealing to the mature babes' brigade for what are quite possibly the same reasons he appeals to the gay guys' group: he's a wild child.

I think they were trying to say that William is "sweet" and Harry is "wild."

My devoted and fabulous friend agrees.

He not only believes it explains the findings; he also believes that absolutely no other explanation is necessary.

5

WHY DO WOMEN WORRY

ABOUT EVERYTHING WHILE MEN

WORRY ABOUT NOTHING?

Women worry more than men.

For example, if a man disagrees with what I just said, he will have absolutely no compunction about letting me know it. A woman will, in contrast, wonder whether she should say anything, ponder whether it would be polite to disagree, question herself about whether it's fair to interrupt and make a contradictory statement.

The guy would have already started to weave the rope he's going to hang me with.

Women don't trust our responses to the world, not even the most basic ones.

No wonder we feel as if we're always pressed for time. We question everything we think, say, and do.

For example, I give a lot of talks to groups where you've got about 300 women in a room. Of these 300 women, at any given time 275 are going to be sweating like barge mules if they're forced, as they inevitably are, to sit in a stuffy hotel ballroom boasting little ventilation and no circulation whatsoever. It's like putting 300 people in a shoe box, only you've given them tiny lined pads and folders with a logo stamped onto the front.

The people who aren't sweating are all under thirty years old and/or weigh less than 115 pounds. They are freezing. Their adorable cable-knit sweaters are pulled tightly across their lithesome narrow shoulders.

The rest of us look like we've just been running with the bulls at Pamplona.

And yet, as the women sit there, wiping perspiration from their brows, fearing that their mascara will melt and that their bras will dampen and become terrarium-like from the condensation formed beneath their moist cleavages, they're all asking each other in fluty voices the eternal question that the first female protozoan asked the second female protozoan: "Is it hot in here, or is it me?"

I'm looking at the audience. I can see that their faces are burning, their cheeks are pink, their mouths are dry; some of them are fanning themselves with a brochure, others are sucking at bottles of water like they just qualified at an Olympic trial. Others look like they're about to slip into heat-induced unconsciousness. Yet nobody is willing to take responsibility for assessing her own microclimate.

This is because we've all learned to be good girls, which was our first mistake.

As good girls, we were taught never to trust ourselves or our own reactions. We can't tell if we're hungry; we only know what we shouldn't eat. We don't know if we're tired; we only know we're not getting enough sleep. We aren't sure that we're fit; we only know we're not sleek. We don't know what our hair color is because we've been dyeing it since we first bought a bottle of Sun-In or henna at age fourteen. Half of us don't know what our weight is because we don't get on a scale. The other half know what our weight is every half hour because we can't get off one.

We get not enough fiber, too much sun, too little calcium, too high a dose of trans fats; we wear shoes that are too small, hats that are too big, panties that leave such deep welts across our waists and buttocks that we look like those dolls who have their underwear permanently embossed across their nether regions for the sake of preserving chastity. (Because every little girl, however naïve, however innocent, knows what kind of undergarment, if any, her doll is wearing. Give a little girl a doll, and the moment she doesn't think anybody is watching, she flips it upside down and, with the authority of an ob/gyn, pulls the dress over its head to check its private parts.)

Women displace our real anxieties onto incidental details.

In search of an example, let's turn back to our sweaty girlfriends in the audience. Why are we just sitting there, literally stewing? Because no woman can imagine herself doing what a man would do, that is to say, walk up to the thermometer and say, "Jesus Christ! It's hot in here. Why the hell don't we turn the air-conditioning on?"

A woman doesn't want to do that because she's afraid that inadvertently she might make somebody else cold: what if one of the little things with the sweater wrapped around her is just getting over the flu? She couldn't risk making somebody else feel bad for her own selfish reasons. It has to be a collective decision, not an individual one. A man, in contrast, thinks, *I'm hot, therefore it must be exceedingly warm in this room. It's probably at least 72.8 degrees.* (Men like to sound scientific and precise even when they make stuff up.)

In contrast, women, caretakers that we are, will try to get a consensus going. Somebody in the back of the room will begin making up one of those charts where you have a spectrum of faces from the smiley one to the frowny one and she'll start telling people to circle whichever best represents their personal comfort level at the moment. She just wants everyone to be part of the decision-making process. "There's no one right answer" is her motto. She sweats all the time.

Of course, it doesn't have to be so complicated; one way that women could lower their body temperatures instantly and effectively and make themselves more comfortable is to remove the jackets they're wearing. This they will never do. To do so would be to reveal their upper arms. After a certain point—for each woman it comes at a different moment—upper-arm exposure is no longer an option.

I know that the right to bare arms did not apply to me after age forty-one. That's when I decided it looked like I had a couple of sausages tied around my neck.

The realization that I could no longer wear cap sleeves was daunting and irreversible, but it coincided neatly with a growing hatred for my elbows.

Elbows offer a whole new body part for a woman to learn to hate, by the way, now that we've been encouraged to focus on the most ridiculous and minute parts of ourselves; witness exfoliating elbow scrubs or diamond-surface heel buffers.

"I have wicked droopy elbows," said my young friend Sarah, who, at twenty-eight, has very little else on her in danger of droopage. "When I straighten my arm, it looks like the curtain going up at the theater." As a young woman facing an uncertain future, Sarah might better spend her time thinking about equal pay for equal work, maintaining a career-family balance, and whether the weakening economy will be able to keep the West's infrastructure intact throughout her lifetime. Instead, she's worrying about the number of pleats on her funny bone.

It's not that I don't understand the impulse. I'm twenty pounds overweight and I worry about the shape of my eyebrows.

So she exfoliates her elbows. If you asked a man the question, "Would you consider exfoliating your elbows?" he would laugh so hard his organs would seize up.

And maybe, just maybe, this whole exfoliating thing has gone too far. One thing I just saw in the store was a terra-cotta loofah. It was like your ordinary loofah, which in non-spa bathroom language we call a sponge and which in the kitchen vernacular is a Brillo pad, only this was made out of baked clay, or what we might call a brick. And I thought to myself, *All right, this is a new low. Can we really be talked into anything by being told it is part of the beauty regime? Will women really do anything to ourselves with any object, however inappropriate, if we're told it will resurface, smooth, vitalize, and rejuvenate? Is there nothing we won't buy?*

In the world of retail, the terra-cotta loofah marketing pitch, I imagine, went something like this:

"Hey, Benny, let's see if we could talk broads into bringing a brick with them into the bathtub. We got them to sit around filing their soft tissue with grit pasted to metal and wearing Scotch tape with toothpaste on their teeth during the day—that was Frankie's best moment, don't you think? The Scotch tape in the mouth routine? I just heard that Home Depot has one hundred and eighty-five boxes of misshapen earthenware with holes in it. Maybe we could tell them it's a loofah and we can tell them it's all natural."

"Harry, you really think that they'll rub themselves with a brick? These are working girls now we're talking about—girls who had a college education, girls who came from good homes."

"Hmm. Maybe you're right. . . . Nope! I got it! We'll tell them it's biodegradable. They'll start buying them as presents for each other. And the great thing is, when they drop them in the bath, they'll break! So they'll have to buy new ones! It's perfect."

"Harry, you're a genius. Let's get a million of 'em. And now let's go ask some younger women out for a drink."

And we women fall for this stuff because we think it's going to make us better. Not just prettier or cuter or more attractive, which, after all, could even be considered legitimate reasons for rubbing a brick on your ass.

No, the sad thing is we actually think this stuff will make us better people.

We do like the idea that it's biodegradable. We do like the idea that the ingredients are all natural (as if we could purchase products made of molecules not found to exist in nature). We think if we smooth our rough edges, grow a second skin, and work our way out of our cocoon, we'll emerge as that butterfly.

It's not like potential sexual partners would notice the details that we spend so much time worrying about. Ironically enough, looking at the ads for plastic surgery is where this becomes abundantly clear. Apparently, now women are having surgery to lift and tighten their earlobes, made saggy by years of being weighed down by all those fabulous baubles they've been forced to wear. I'm sorry, but if you're worrying about your earlobes and whether they're giving your age away, you should get yourself a day job, or at the very least another haircut.

This is not something a man would do. Have you looked at the ears of a man over forty?

First of all, that's quite a silly question. Of course you've looked at the ears of a man over forty because you can't avoid them. They're huge. They're like speakers coming out of the sides of his head. They're like satellite dishes with those big wires coming out of them, perhaps to improve reception. Not to mention the hairs growing out of their noses like some kind of nasal brand of Chia Pet. (And they're probably going to make Chia Pets out of those terra-cotta loofahs they don't sell: "Look, Harry, women can make pets out of these. They can grow herbs." "Better than that, Benny: catnip! We'll make the crazy cat ladies buy them. After all, they're organic.")

Women have been taught to repress all of our bodily functions. When a guy's stomach starts to make noise, he makes an announcement: "Whoa! Shouldn't've had that second piece of pepperoni," he says. Then he rubs his belly with pride. If a woman makes the slightest gurgle, she slinks off as though she's about to calve.

If a guy has something stuck between his teeth, he'll keep talking with his tongue stuck up into his gums and try to suck the morsel out without giving up his ascendant role in the conversation, whereas a woman will excuse herself, go the restroom, unearth the floss that she carries in those little convenient Y-shaped configurations that resemble nothing so much as tiny IUDs (perhaps to be used for those dolls who don't have the underwear embossed on their undersides), and return with freshly applied lipstick and lip liner.

If a guy has something hanging precipitously out of one of his nostrils, his friends will find this so amusing, they will take photographs of him with their cell phones and e-mail them to everyone on their network before letting the victim know, whereupon he will use a neatly pressed, monogrammed handkerchief (if he is over forty) to correct the situation, or take a picture of himself with his own cell phone (if he is under forty) while stating reassuringly to the company, "Got it." A woman in the exact same situation would simply have to set herself on fire once it was pointed out to her, which would be done by other women who, in unison, would all start rubbing their own noses in code and in sympathy for the victim.

Like baseball umpires, women have a whole underground language to express to other women how they're messed up. If one woman starts wiping under her eyes to check on her mascara while talking to another woman, the other woman will also start rubbing under her eyes. The two of them will look like sad lemmings, imitating each other before heading toward the cliff.

If a woman checks her bra strap, you can bet that every one of her colleagues around the table is going to figure out how to check her own. If a woman puts her index finger up to her mouth and seems to be correcting something near her lip area, every woman with whom she's made eye contact in the last minute is going to assume that there's a crumb the size of a schnauzer on her own upper lip. And it is one of life's few certainties that if a woman brushes imaginary dandruff off her shoulder, every woman is going to brush off her own shoulders in a gesture so similar it would seem as if they're all in a chorus line.

Women see other women as mirrors of ourselves, especially if that mirror can be considered unflattering.

We see a woman with stringy hair and we vow to change our conditioner. We see a woman with visible panty lines and we start wearing Spanx (steel-reinforced foundation undergarments more or less advertised as "not your mother's girdle" when the real motto should be "when you don't want your butt to look like your father's Oldsmobile").

We see someone around our age who, in wearing an ivory ensemble, does not look like a breath of spring but instead like a wheel of Brie; we are disturbed when we notice a woman wearing an elegant knit suit who doesn't look like an elegant powerhouse but instead resembles a stuffed sock.

And it's not that we're judging these women as somehow sabotaging themselves but more that we see in them a possible reflection of our own shortcomings. We see the eyelifts, eyebrow shaping, chin molding, earplasty, and gel nails and we either smile inwardly at the aplomb with which these are carried off or wince with inner wonder at the pervasive question "Does she have any idea what she looks like?"

We ask this in full sympathy, because we know in our heart of hearts, we know—of course we know—she has no idea.

We know that because we *know* we have no idea what we look like. Just the way we have no idea if it's hot in here, or if it's us.

6

DOES YOUR CUP RUNNETH OVER?

Like Scarlett O'Hara with a fist raised to heaven, you make a solemn vow: you *will* get a bra that fits perfectly.

This will never happen.

Not even if you are a woman.

Not that I'm bitter, but there is no perfect bra.

How do I know? If there were a perfect brassiere, women around the globe would be telephoning, yelling over backyard fences, e-mailing, sending smoke signals—anything—to alert other women that the quest has proved fruitful at last. (Wasn't there a troubadour ballade titled "Les Femmes dans le quest pour la brassiere parfaite"? I believe it's in *The Bedford Introduction to Literature*.) The ideal ur-bra having been discovered is not information a self-respecting member of the sisterhood would keep to herself.

Most women have two breasts and twenty-seven brassieres.

Something's wrong with these numbers.

I once bought a cheap brassiere ($12.95) in 1997 and it fit perfectly, but the manufacturers stopped making that model as soon as they knew I liked it.

Some of us were part of the generation that decided bras were evidence of the patriarchy's worn-out, not to say lopsided, stance on the need to repress and contain women's bodies. Many of us decided that, unlike our mothers and grandmothers, we would not shove and stuff our flesh inside girdles and corsets as if we were made of Play-Doh and could be molded at will. We felt just fine wearing T-shirts, thank you, with nothing between us and our front pockets (pockets that were strategically placed because The Fear of Visible Nipples still lurked).

After the famous poster of Farrah Fawcett from the mid-seventies, however, pockets were no longer de rigueur; even cheerleader types could kill their Living Bras.

There are still battles to be fought in terms of gaining full equality for women, and the battle of the bra remains a small (don't even try to make a joke here, I'm warning you) but significant one.

Turns out that the culture is, yes, still trying to get women to control our bodies in order to meet men's fantasies in terms of beauty. That is bad. What is worse—it becomes clear after wearing brassieres for thirty years—is that women's underwear was clearly designed by men. By the same bunch who gave us stiletto heels. By the same group who designed automatically self-destructing panty hose. By the same geniuses who encouraged us to start thinking that we were insufficiently feminine if we did not get bikini waxes. As if "bring forth children in pain" were not enough, we must inflict anguish upon ourselves whenever possible in order to be a real girl.

So what, in the bra arena, can a girl do?

You can, of course, resign yourself to buying big old white brassieres from a catalog, the ones that hoist your breasts up and practically swing them over your shoulders.

But even these, ugly as they are, are far from perfect. You have to match them with Grandma panties, for one thing. You can't wear a big honking white four-hook bra and a silk thong. That's for specialists; some people get paid extra for donning that outfit, and it's nothing you should try at home.

So we search for cute bras.

Cute bras will look cute as long as they do not actually touch your person. Even when you gather up enough courage to be measured by the official Lingerie Lady (aka "Ilsa of the SS"), you end up leaving with a garment as useless as it is heartbreaking.

My extensive research shows that bras fit their wearers for the first fifteen minutes, whereupon they partake of the "shrink-wrap" effect. Body temperatures cause the elastic in the shoulder straps to wither and tighten, causing uncontrollable itching in the middle of your back. Parts of your person that have never poufed out before will grow, muffin-like, and spill over the edge of the cute bra. You begin to look not unlike a segmented insect.

Front-closure bras, while a good idea, have the unfortunate tendency to pop, thereby causing your breasts to fling themselves onto the dinner plate.

Sometimes not even your own dinner plate.

Sports bras are great, but they look funny under formal wear.

What can professional expertise offer? The following passage is lifted directly from a manufacturer's Web site: "Add 5 to the measurement (i.e., if 'A is 29,' the back size is 34). After 33 inches, only add 3 inches to the back measurement (i.e., if 'A is 35,' the back size is 38). This measurement should equal your back size calculation. For example, if you measured 29 inches around your rib cage, the calculation is $29 + 5 = 34$."

If I could do that kind of math, I wouldn't be sitting here trying to figure out my cup size. I would be solving the mysteries of the universe. Or at the very least topping up my already sizable portfolio, the profits of which I would have been able to bank on because I was good at figures.

If I were very good at figures, I wouldn't have to worry so much about mine.

If I had that kind of money, I would simply buy whatever Scarlett O'Hara was wearing.

Even when she raised her fist into the air, her bra was perfect.

7

HOW CAN A "GIFT" *NOT* BE FREE?

When feeling oppressed by domesticity and the straightjacket of gender expectations, men and women often respond differently: men will start wars, buy cars, or go to Hooters.

Women will get themselves a little treat.

I was shopping last week and I decided to indulge in my gender-specific stress-reducing activity. I made a self-indulgent purchase. I bought something just for me. (And since I hate using that kind of cutesy phrase, you can see just how frazzled I already was even before I embarked on this mission; I was shopping because I had three deadlines and I needed to do something—anything—other than write.)

Anyway, I like to buy makeup—not because I believe that the indulgence in girly-girl femininity acts as a fabulous cultural counterpart to the edgy intellectual feminism that has emerged since the new millennium. I buy makeup because I'm an idiot.

But something new happened during this most recent consumer transaction.

When I got the makeup home, I got mad.

And not for the usual reasons (among the usual reasons would be the fact that the lipstick that looked scarlet at the store turns out to be tangerine; the fact that a new mascara profoundly irritates my eyes so that I weep copious sooty tears; the fact that the foundation, when applied, does not make my face luminous but instead makes it look as if it's been inexpertly spackled).

No, the concealed and powerful weapon encased in the faux-lizard lavender-colored bag was disguised as a gift. The instructions enclosed suggested that the small "extra" item should be used as a gift for a friend. Never before had I wanted to throw a cosmetic item into a roaring fire. Never before had I wanted to throttle somebody who worked in the marketing department of a corporation.

What do they mean, I should give this to somebody as a gift? Suddenly the makeup company is trying to run my intimate life? Bad enough lingerie ads encourage women to buy push-up bras for their husbands (if their husbands want to wear push-up bras, let them go get fitted and deal with the underwear biting into their torsos).

But now some makeup maven is encroaching on my sororal friendships? I just spent the whole damn day and my whole last paycheck buying things for other people. I don't want to be told in a pamphlet that I should give something of my own away in order to understand the joys of giving. Most women I know don't need any encouragement to enjoy the joys of giving. We need to be encouraged to experience the joys of making ourselves happy. That's what we do far too infrequently.

Almost no woman would treat any of her acquaintances as poorly as she treats herself.

Consider this: can you imagine marketing people trying to pull this on a guy?

Seriously, can you even imagine a guy buying two pairs of pants on sale and finding a note in the pocket saying: "Why don't you give this to a good friend?" Buying a Phillips-head screwdriver and being instructed to give the attached socket wrench to a buddy? Yeah, that'd go over real big.

I'd like to see them try. Please, please, let someone try. And then let me and my friends watch.

Guys would answer back.

Women aren't brought up to answer back, and sometimes we need to answer back. We need to establish ourselves. Now, one of my favorite answering-back lines comes from Liz Carpenter, during those days when she was working for the Johnson administration and wrote a book called *Ruffles and Flourishes*. It did really well. So Liz Carpenter, first female Press Secretary to a First Lady, not a shy girl by nature, is at a big Washington party. Arthur Schlesinger Jr., the historian, comes up to her and in this "just kidding, come on, honey, can't you take a joke?" sort of way says, "Loved your book, Liz. Who wrote it for you?"

Now, as a good girl—which as you can tell is a project I've personally abandoned despite being brought up that way—your first response is to go, "Ahh, I don't understand why you're trying to undermine my work. I put so much of myself into this book, and now you're just trying to make fun of it." And a good girl's voice, earnestly defending herself, goes up so high that only a sub-species of rain-forest bats can hear it. That is not a good sign.

So what Liz Carpenter does—and this is the part that makes her my heroine—is when Schlesinger comes up and says, "Loved your book, Liz. Who wrote it for you?" she instantly replies, "Glad you liked it, Arthur. Who read it to you?"

I still love that answer. I worship it because it says, "You know what, honey? If we're gonna play, we're both gonna play."

It's not like this guy just tossed a medicine ball at this woman and now she puts it in her seven-hundred-pound bag and drags it with her.

Because when somebody says something like "who wrote it for you?" what do you do?

If you're a normal person, you're lying awake in the middle of the night staring at the ceiling. You have a notepad next to the bed. You're writing down what you should have said, right? You're muttering, "Next time, I'm gonna say this, and then I'm gonna say that, and I'm going to be looking fabulous when I say it, and I'm going to be doing this."

Now, lying awake at two o'clock in the morning is not going to help you.

You have to get rid of the nagging unsaid lines. We can do this by actually saying them.

We all need to spend time getting rid of those voices that stop us from being ourselves; we have to smack down the voices that say, *Don't answer back; they won't like you.* I mean, you've got to get that answer out, because there are answers that if you don't get out, they just sit there. That's a violation of yourself; when you don't say what needs to be said, it does not go away.

It is like nuclear waste, sinking into the ground: you might not see it, but it doesn't leave, and it poisons everything else. So that if you don't answer back when you need to, the next time somebody just gives you a perfectly nice "hey, baby" on the street, you get out an AK-47, because you didn't answer back the guy who said, "Who wrote it for you?"

So we need to get our real responses out there, we need to be able to tell the truth about our lives, but what's interesting about this is men who are in the room will say, "I could never think of that."

But women only will come up and say, "Let's say a miracle occurred—a miracle occurred—and I could think of that. I would still be up at two o'clock in the morning."

I'd say, "Why?"

They say, "I'd be up at two o'clock in the morning thinking, *Oh my God, what if Arthur Schlesinger Jr. is secretly illiterate? What if he has a child who's dyslexic? What if he has a grandchild using* Hooked on Phonics?"

Then they would have to volunteer two nights a week for the Literacy Society of America, for once having opened their mouth. I don't think so. I think that, in fact, if women stopped apologizing for everything we do and everything we think, we could have a lot more time in our lives. We could reorganize the government. Write books.

Get ourselves a few little treats.

8

WHO ARE YOU CALLING

A SECOND WIFE?

I never expected to be a second wife. No one does; no little girl longs to grow up and walk down the aisle to the strains of "Here Comes the Second Bride, All Dressed in an Ivory Suit." But here I am, married to a man who was married before, wrapped up in his life and the lives of his children, and related in some bizarre fashion without a name (spouse-in-law?) to the woman he married straight out of college.

Getting married to a man who has been married before has all the disadvantages of a time-share, and few of the carefree pleasures.

Yet as a second wife, I believe that I'm the *REAL* wife. I'm not the required course but the elective, the selection he made as an adult. He left his first wife. He divorced her and, a couple of years later, married me.

That's the simple chronology. The story is more complicated.

Although I was not the reason for the dissolution of my husband's first marriage, I am regarded as the occasion, especially by some of his old compatriots who were hunting for reasons to condemn him. "Why would any man go through the whole miserable mess of a divorce—only to get married again?" they gasped in astonishment and disbelief.

His male friends were genuinely puzzled. His female friends were annoyed.

His accountant was extremely nervous.

They wanted to know one thing: how did I get him to do it?

As if the key to a second marriage is some type of concealed sexual weapon.

Quite simply, I am the grown-up woman he married as a grown-up man. It's not a series of glittering evenings drinking martinis in smoky bars. Instead, it is the familiar routine of waking to an arm around your waist, the companionable bathroom talk with mouths full of toothpaste, and the idea that someone will know if you don't make it home at night. Yet even though we are galloping into our tenth year of marriage, I am still considered The Second One by certain of our acquaintances.

Let's face it: Not many people like a second wife. Not the wives of college friends, not old relatives who can't remember new names but who remember that they shelled out good money for a fancy gift the first time around, and especially not the original wife, who thinks of herself as the bona fide wife.

But when a man marries for the second time he knows what he's getting into. He enters willingly, eyes open, arms spread—a skydiver. Emerging broken, bruised, and bleeding from a previous fall when the parachute didn't *quite* open, he is nevertheless willing to do it again and at an even greater risk; everyone knows second marriages are risky.

The surprise is this: when the moment comes, the man jumps with alacrity.

So why is the phrase "second wife" so unnerving? When even used-car dealers don't regard themselves as purveyors of second-hand merchandise, when secondhand clothes stores are now consignment shops, why should I stick with the second-wife moniker? It's not like *I* wasn't married before, too. My husband is as much a second husband as I'm a second wife. In part, this is due to the fact that there is still a contingent for which a marriage without children is only slightly more honorable than a series of one-night stands. Yet we make as felicitous a stepfamily as you are likely to find.

Being a second wife and a stepmother is rather like a set of aerial maneuvers. There *are* seriously complicated stunts involved— trapeze artists have less difficulty in learning when to disappear and resurface at exactly the right moments than your average second wife.

And there remains a slight sense of imbalance. His first marriage counted. My first marriage—even though it lasted five years—did not. During my final two years in my first marriage, I was constantly telling my friends how I wanted to make my relationship work. Then I learned that marriages aren't like cars, independent of the people in them, to be fixed according to an owner's manual.

Nevertheless, I still do what second wives inevitably do: I've counted the years until he will have been married to me longer than he was to her. The equation works against me. If that's the only way marriages are judged, I might lose. But it can't just be about going the distance, like two fighters who claim victory because they're still standing, bloodied and incoherent, when the final bell rings.

Call me romantic, but surely a union can't be considered successful simply because it exists over a lengthy period of time until one of the partners is officially "departed" and drops to the ground like a gargoyle falling off a rotting building?

I realized a couple of years after I remarried that one of my oldest friends never quite forgave me for getting on with life after my divorce. Treating me with the resentment of a union official watching a house being constructed with nonunion labor, my erstwhile friend watched me build up and remodel my life. She has never absolved me from the sin of being happy.

To sum up: I am married to a man I love and am lucky. We'd both been married before, but does that really matter? Should second wives post billboards proclaiming that we are not necessarily women who flounce through life wearing ankle bracelets, feather boas, and alligator shoes? As some statistics have it, we are one in every four married women you will meet.

So why there isn't any official "us" to those of us who are second wives? Why is there no architectural blueprint, or map, of our position? Is it because no woman believes she will ever actually *be* in our position? Or is it because we have to shake off the stigma attached to being The Second Wife and say, with a smile, "Yes indeed, I'm his second wife. But I'm his last."

9

WHY DO THEY CALL IT A GLASS CEILING WHEN IT'S REALLY JUST A THICK LAYER OF MEN?

You'll hear from everyone—relatives, friends, strangers on the subway wearing paper plates for hats—that it's women who sabotage other women in the workplace. Me, I don't think so. More than twenty years of professional experience has proved to me that indeed there are men out there who don't make life easier for women at work.

I know, I know: this comes as a *big* shock.

Call me crazy—and I am willing to explore the idea that I am actually the only one who has ever had this revelation—but I believe there is an entirely non-organized, non-conspiratorial group I'd nevertheless like to bracket together under one aegis and call Guys We Don't Like To Work With (GWDLTWW).

I believe GWDLTWW should be thinned from the herd. We

need to recognize them and weed them out. At least, that's my girlish way of looking at things.

In brief, this is how to decide if you're working with one of them:

1. When they have not prepared sufficiently, GWDLTWW are more overbearing and talkative than usual in order to compensate for what they know to be their inadequacy. If such a man keeps asking questions about one particular paragraph and raising complex philosophical issues about it, you can bet that he's only read the paragraph and wants to hide behind that tiny piece of information like a six-hundred-pound wrestler trying to hide behind a washrag. What to remember is this: if there's a guy on your committee who won't shut up about the report, you can bet he hasn't read the report.

2. GWDLTWW will stand in front of your desk and ask if you have gum, candy, soda, muffins, cigarettes, a lighter, a stapler, a Band-Aid, extra paper, Post-it notes, Advil, or Kleenex. They think of every woman as, basically, a bodega. They think that every woman not only carries all the supplies they'd ever need but also believes she should offer products and services on the spot and with a smile.

3. GWDLTWW read over your shoulder, finish your sentences, and consider it their duty to correct you when they think you're wrong, which is much of the time. They love when you make tiny mistakes, just as some women—not your friends, of course—love to tell you that you have lipstick on your teeth or a run in your tights. These GWDLTWW are not like reg-

ular people who will tell you that you have lipstick on your teeth in a discreet way but will instead announce, "Danielle, are your gums bleeding or is that lipstick?" in a voice as loud as but more clear than the conductor announcing the next stop on the IRT.

4. GWDLTWW, when giving instructions for something they consider important, inevitably speak to you as if you're s-l-o-w or simultaneously translating their words into your native tongue; they will occasionally pause to see if you comprehend their message the way a stage hypnotist might make his head rear back to emphasize his magical powers. When taking instructions from you, GWDLTWW look at their nails, sigh, and say, "Yes, yes, I already know. It's fine, okay? Not to worry." (NB: if they say, "No problemo," do please fire them.)

5. No matter what happens, GWDLTWW never, ever, ever admit that they're wrong. If you say to one, "Gee, the entire infrastructure of the corporation is collapsing because of your mismanaged division," he says, "Well, you should have seen what it looked like before I got here," or, "If we were working within a righteous and fair system, I wouldn't have been put in such an untenable position in the first place, not to mention the fact that I'm sure my administrative assistant just got knocked up by her deadbeat boyfriend—our hiring practices have been unsound for quite some time." He never thinks that "unsound hiring practices" refers to him.

6. GWDLTWW treat everyone with what they see as a sense of detached and razor-sharp irony but themselves become very sensitive when criticized or even observed closely (which

amounts to the same thing). When one of these guys perceives a piece of criticism coming close to being sniffed out in public, he becomes terribly earnest and looks at the perpetrator of the atrocity—otherwise known as the person disagreeing with him—as if she were the mother who left him at day care before he was ready. In this situation GWDLTWW suddenly adopt the defense strategy of the New Man, to the point where they become All Quiet, even while they somehow manage to pout audibly—their lower lip sticking out so far you can hear it quiver.

7. The GWDLTWW will paint a portrait of any woman who says anything aside from "What a brilliant idea" and "Wow! I never would have thought of that" as a man-hating, disenfranchised, lonely, probably alcoholic, bitter spinster (or dominatrix, or ex-wife) with a second-rate mind. If you ask such a man to discuss whether he has any issues with your work or management style, he will simply make light of it when talking to you but will then add "paranoia" and "narcissism" to your list of character traits.

8. GWDLTWW love to have debates, until they start to lose; then they have to get to a meeting.

9. GWDLTWW mention their children constantly, as if to prove that they are nurturing, scrapbooking, compassionate individuals who can basically understand everything that every woman has ever gone through—after all, he knows what women's lives are like—who doesn't? Such a man covers his desk with pictures of his kids as small children, even if those kids have now graduated from business school.

10. GWDLTWW think that if you are not speaking, or if you are sitting quietly, then you need to be given a task. A silent woman to them is like a blank sheet of paper that they need to doodle on.

11. When GWDLTWW sign up to do a project with a woman, they automatically assume that their role will be advisory and consultative. If there's Xeroxing to be done or lists to be compiled, they'd be grateful if she could get a copy of these to them by 4:00 P.M.

12. GWDLTWW walk faster.

13. They nod and smile less.

14. They never apologize. (See "GWDLTWW never, ever, ever admit that they're wrong" earlier.)

15. They never bring the muffins (although they will offer to pay for them).

16. GWDLTWW check women's math.

17. GWDLTWW will only let a woman borrow their handkerchief if she is under thirty and weighs less than 118 pounds.

18. GWDLTWW will sabotage female co-workers by pretending to be interested in stories of their personal lives, all the while chronicling their emotional fluctuations with the same careful attention that someone on the trading floor keeps an eye on the NASDAQ. These men will save this information to use against the women later: "Well, Angela, we know how fragile you are when things are stressed at home—remember when you were having so much trouble sleeping last summer? Bad times, right?—so maybe Skip here should handle the new account."

19. GWDLTWW will quote from *The Iliad, The Art of War, The Prince*, and/or *The Tipping Point* as if they wrote them or were best friends with one of the authors.
20. GWDLTWW will swear in front of women to see if it makes them uncomfortable.
21. GWDLTWW use the word "feminization" the way the more enthusiastic members of Spanish Inquisition used the word "demonization."
22. GWDLTWW always take the chairs with arms.
23. GWDLTWW never clean the coffeepot. They never even shut it off.

10

WHO'S FUNNIER?

If you're looking for a good time, you're better off in the world of *I Love Lucy, The Simpsons,* and *The Honeymooners* than you are in the company of the snooty people on *Gossip Girl, Beverly Hills 90210,* or *Desperate Housewives.*

My big Italian family was funny. And we were poor, which is why I am comfortable saying the poor are funnier than the rich. You had to be funny in our neighborhood or else you couldn't survive; you had to learn to "crack wise," to make yourself heard above the sound of your aunt Josephine whacking a cutlet with a wooden mallet like John Henry laying down track. If our humor was vulgar—bathroom humor, slyly suggestive sexual innuendo, or the irreverent mocking of social norms—well, that's because we were basically prototypes for The Vulgar.

For example, because I was the first girl in my family to go to college (or to graduate from high school in a timely fashion), my aunts were suspicious when I said I was going to school in New Hampshire. They assumed I was pregnant. Why else would I have to leave the neighborhood? I was the only freshman at Dartmouth whose family expected her home after nine months.

"That one has a mouth on her" was one way my family described me. "She has no shame" was the other way (this while I was standing there—my family always referred to people in the third person, as if the individual under discussion was deaf or invisible or both). It wasn't just me my family was describing. "A big mouth" and "no shame" are pretty much the hallmarks of all working-class comedy.

By "big mouth" I mean not only a sizable vocal orifice but also a penchant for constant, loud, impolite talk. Uncensored talk. Honest talk, even when honesty is rude. Big mouths are the ones yelling, "Hey! The Emperor has no clothes!"

Big mouths, when they make smart and honest observations, cause trouble. From Groucho to Whoopi to Nicole Hollander's *Sylvia* comic strip—from Brett Butler to George Lopez to Dave Chappelle—the prevailing focus of working-class humor is the examination of what it feels like to be part of a subordinate group within a society that prides itself on egalitarianism and fair play.

This leads us to the "no shame" part of the equation. It's tough to have shame when the whole family lives in four rooms. Living in close quarters, you cannot escape that people possess bodies. You have *pasta e fagioli,* you have gas; what's the big deal? You have one toilet in the house? Then you take a number, like at a bakery.

A lot of comedy is about lack of privacy, and the poor have a lock on that (because they can't put locks on anything else). Everything is public, open, and available for inspection.

Another reason the poor have no shame (and a great deal of resilience) is because they have little to lose. They pick up what they can where they find it, even if the more privileged observer might not see it. The poor forage for humor, hunt and gather it, which means they get it in its raw state. It's more delicious, fresher, and because it is free there's a lot of it to go around. It's also sometimes a little rougher, maybe tougher to digest. Not possessing much, ironically, gives them a freedom and independence that the rich, fearful of losing the trappings of privilege and of power, cannot afford. If the nannied rich have to hiss, "Not in front of the servants," when they behave badly, the poor do not have to worry about keeping up appearances.

The rich can less afford to be funny because power is so closely associated with dignity. It's one of the reasons that the independent film *The Aristocrats* found such a wide audience. As one reviewer put it, the film "is a working demonstration of the pleasures of the profane." When you can make use of the profane while attacking the privileged, you have an explosive combination.

Which makes it easy to see why so many comics take aim at the ruling classes: authentically edgy comedy wants to shake things up. That's one of the reasons so many of the newer voices in comedy emerge from various "outsider" groups.

Some are alternatively sexualized (which is the only way I can think to describe the brilliant Eddie Izzard, my new heartthrob who just happens to wear a dress); some will be part of two distinct cultures and eager to comment on both (such as Shazia Mirza, a self-described moderate, devout Muslim, who regards the "whole point" of her stand-up comedy as being "to help reduce Islamophobia"). Issues of class are inevitably mixed with issues of sex, gender, and race, and pretty much any performer who isn't Conan O'Brien, Jerry Seinfeld, or Steve Martin is going to see that the powers that be deserve a lack of tenderness.

Everybody wants to laugh at the ruling class. The secret lives of those with inherited money and power enthrall us because we suspect that they are feeble and weird. Their inner lives are private, classified, unlike ours, and so when earthy humorists expose the sophisticated classes as loony or corrupt, our hopes are confirmed.

That's because so many of them are about ourselves. Comic Jeff Foxworthy: "If your watchband is wider than any book you've ever read, you might be a redneck." The same holds true "if you have a full set of salad bowls and they all say 'Cool Whip' on the side."

Another Blue-Collar Comedy Tour comic, Larry the Cable Guy, offers the following: "I got a vasectomy at Sears. When I get excited, the garage door opens," crafting a joke out of the very elements that have made country music popular: sexual matters and vehicles (and vehicular accessories). Adding "Sears" to the mix tweaks it perfectly, along the same lines as a classic Roseanne bit: "I'll start doing housework when Sears invents a riding vacuum cleaner." Replacing "Sears" with "Restoration Hardware" would not have a comparable comic effect.

Contrast that kind of humor with the kind found in the

supremely narcissistic personal essays read regularly on National Public Radio, inevitably followed by music from a reed instrument.

The powerless classes, by virtue of being powerless, have a built-in comic view of the world. They can make fun of themselves and their "betters" without damaging their position (which is nonexistent anyway). It comes with the territory; it's a viewpoint. You either have it or you don't. And if you have a whole lot of inherited dough, then you probably don't. Don't feel too bad—after all, you have everything else.

In an unfair world (what other kind is there?) where you can secure a fancy education if your family has enough money (remember the line from *The Wizard of Oz:* "I can't give you a brain, but I can give you a diploma"?), where you can buy beauty through fitness, cosmetics, and, if all else fails, plastic surgery, where you can even learn to imitate sympathy, compassion, and affection through the use of letter templates or the wholesale acquisition of greeting cards, isn't it sort of great that you can't steal or buy shares of humor? Maybe that's why, when it comes to being funny, the poor will always have an edge.

Women are funny. We are certainly funnier than men. Which is why you always hear laughter coming from the women's room—we're having a riot in there.

You rarely hear laughter coming from the men's room. And the fact that they don't have separate stalls is only *part* of the reason.

Put three women together for more than three minutes and—whether or not they have ever met before—they will have exchanged vital details of their inner lives and started to laugh. Sit next to a woman for lunch and you'll know whether she's in a relationship, if that relationship is any good, whether she has kids, whether the kids are happy, and whether we now like the woman her father started to date after her mother died last year. If you sit next to a woman for an entire *dinner,* you'll know whether she's taking estrogen orally, through a patch, or using an herbal mix provided by a naturopath.

Guys aren't like this. Most of their conversations consist of asking each other questions that can be answered numerically. Men can play poker together for twenty-two years and know precisely two things about their comrades: their first names and what kinds of cars they drive. They spend their time at the card game chortling at each other's defeats and telling each other jokes—not because they want to amuse their companions, but because they want to win the joke competition.

Humorous interaction between men instantly becomes a joke-off.

Women don't joke-off that way.

You'll notice, in fact, that women rarely tell jokes; instead we tell stories.

We move from gritty details of intimate life to the generalities of politics and culture within a single sentence. We use humor to name things in our lives the world wants to keep mysterious. Comic Pam Stone has a great story about this: "I had a girlfriend who told me she was in the hospital for female problems. I said, 'Get real! What does that mean?' She says, 'You know, *female* problems.' I said, 'What? You can't parallel park? You can't get credit?'"

Using humor to bridge gaps in conversation and in our lives was illustrated for me most poignantly as I waited on line at the local all-night Stop & Shop. It was nearly midnight and the place looked like a cross between a hospital and an airport in an Eastern Bloc country: huge, clean, and empty; there were a few people in uniforms and a few lost souls trying to get home.

I stood behind a woman whom I'd never met but who was, from all appearances, my match. In my cart were milk, juice, cereal, peaches, and kitty litter. Basics. In contrast, hers had filet mignon, baking potatoes, sour cream, fresh parsley—the works. As she started placing these on the belt at the register, I leaned over and said with half a laugh, "Excuse me, but can I go home with you? This looks like one great meal."

Looking me straight in the eye as she counted out some tangerines, she said without missing a beat, "It's for tomorrow night's dinner. If *we don't decide to move in together* tomorrow night, it's over."

Now, I'd never met her before, but of course I knew exactly what she meant and could supply, in the shorthand of all female existence everywhere, all the necessary information.

"How long has it been?" I asked.

"Five years," she replied, arching an eyebrow for effect as I nodded. "I'm forty-four years old," she continued. "If I'm going to learn to live with another adult it had better be *now*."

Meanwhile, the woman working the register starts ringing up the steak and says, "Honey, sounds like a bad deal to me. You've been on your own and you've liked it, because otherwise you would have hooked up with somebody. Trust me. This way you can have a relationship without all the attendant garbage of cohabitation. You have any coupons?" She says this as she expertly scans the produce under the magic green eye that records the price. She knows what everything costs, including, it seems, the relationship under discussion. By now we are all double-bagging the groceries and talking at the same time. We are laughing, but the laughter underscores—yet in no way undermines—the gravity of the story.

Even though there is no follow-up memo, even though we do not know each other's names, we know this is real work, the telling of our tales; the turning of anxiety into humor is the equivalent of spinning straw into gold. We take it seriously.

Our funny stories are about our actual lives, about trying to stay sane in a society where forty-five-year-old women try to fit into jeans they wore in high school and weep when they can't, for example. About surviving a world where making seventy-eight cents on a man's dollar is considered "a pretty good deal"—and is used as evidence of the inexorable feminization of the culture. The ironies of life are not hard to find.

Men insult each other as a way of bonding. They mock, cruelly, the physical flaws of other men. Men will go up to a very handsome guy, for example, who happens to have lost his hair (and he's probably looked everywhere for it, too) and by way of friendly greeting say, "Hey, Fat Jack, can you shine that dome up a little bit? I've got something in my eye and I've got to get it out."

You have never heard a woman go up to another woman and say the equivalent kind of thing. Women do not go up to other women and say, "Mary, three months pregnant or going heavy on the gravy?"

We don't do that.

We have our own meaningless rituals, of course. If two women haven't seen each other in more than twenty minutes you'll hear them exclaim, "Ah! Gloria! You look wonderful! What did you do with your hair?"

Now what's fascinating to me is that Gloria, in the history of Western culture, has never been known to say "thank you" when being given a compliment. We don't do that, either. We will argue with you about why your compliment is wrong.

(Actually, when I give talks, men from the audience tell me all the time, "I'm afraid to compliment women." It's not because they're afraid of a lawsuit. It's because they don't want a twenty-minute explanation of why the woman they've just flattered doesn't look good.)

Anyway, you'll hear a woman shouting, "Gloria, I love what you did with your hair!" And Gloria will respond by saying, in all horror, "Are you *kidding*? Look, in the back." Here Gloria will bend over and flip her hair up to prove her point. "Look, look, look. No, look, I paid sixty-five dollars, and look, look, look."

If you go up to a woman and say, "Marcia, nice jacket," you won't hear "thank you." You'll hear: "On sale. T.J. Maxx. I bought it on Memorial Day, twenty percent off. I have the card. I get five percent back. But look, I look like a house, look, look."

That's what we do.

Our humor is both public and private. We exchange information for the purpose of helping one another—wherever we happen to be. Consider this story about Tallulah Bankhead: In a public restroom during an intermission Tallulah discovered that there was no toilet paper. "I beg your pardon, but do you have any toilet tissue in your cubicle?" she asked her neighbor. Receiving a negative reply, Tallulah tried again: "Do you have any Kleenex perhaps?" Again, the reply was negative. "Not even some cotton wool? A piece of wrapping paper?" A long pause followed the third negative, after which could be heard the sound of a purse opening. Tallulah's resigned drawl finally came through the partition: "Darling, do you have two fives for a ten?"

Women's humor is not for the fainthearted or the easily shocked. But then again, neither is waking up in the morning. Nobody said life would be easy. What I'm saying is that it can, at the very least, be fun. By seeing the ironies and absurdities of the world around us we can lighten up and be less weighed down—humor permits perspective, and perspective is essential for change.

There is something clarifying, redemptive, and vital about using humor; dead serious is no way to go through life.

So make some trouble and laugh out loud. And always have two fives for a ten.

11

WHY DO WE ENVY OTHERS?

(LIKE THERE'S ANYBODY ELSE

TO ENVY?)

When faced by the success of a good friend, why do we often hear a scratchy inner voice saying, *Does she really deserve that?*

Is it just envy that makes us feel this way? Or is there something more sophisticated, darker, more complex, more intricate, woven into this design?

Remember how Bottom in *A Midsummer Night's Dream* wants to play all the characters in the play-within-a-play? Bottom wants to claim the roles of Lion, Wall, and Moonlight, and insists that he should be permitted to show his talents from every perspective. His exaggerated willingness, his intense desire, his frantic need to be all things to all people is what makes him comic.

Very funny, right? Big laugh.

The wish to be everything or have everything possessed by our friends, however, can be a little less funny when life is played off the stage.

Isn't there somewhere inside of us where we all wonder, *Why did she get this and I didn't? Why does he like her better than he likes me? How come she got a raise? Why did she get a grant, he get a promotion, they get books with Oxford/Harvard/Norton/Chicago/Palgrave? Why didn't I find that dress on sale?*

Certainly this is true in our professional lives. Be honest now. Don't you want to feel just a little smug by the time you finish reading this? Aren't you hoping to find a few faults (or continental divides) with my argument?

Every writer I know is secretly miserable when faced with a glowing review of another writer's work, especially if that other writer is an acquaintance (defined as someone you have met at perhaps three events during, say, the past seventeen years). One friend who would set me on fire if I used his name put it succinctly: "I can't read *The New York Times Book Review* anymore. I have to have my wife remove it from the paper before I can even pick it up and start reading other sections. Even when there's nothing of mine to be reviewed, it somehow irritates me that these papers are filled with praise for somebody else."

Let's face it: it remains vaguely unsatisfactory when a colleague who is more successful, although, perhaps, less talented, offers, by way of reassurance, "Oh, I just got lucky." To such unsatisfactory remarks it's almost impossible to resist saying, "Damn right it's unfair! It should have been me, not you." What's to say that making such remarks out loud is not a way to make friends and influence people? So we bottle these remarks up inside.

Here's another example, even closer to home: I envy women who have adorable toddlers. When I see a mother with a curly-headed little tike who's wearing pink Oshkosh overalls, I can barely contain myself. When they're walking through the mall and waving at a teddy bear in the toy-store window, my envy knows no bounds.

But when I overhear these same women in the ladies' rooms pleading for the kid to "do it for Mummy," my instinct is to back away immediately. I absolutely believe my instinct confirms that had I been in charge of raising the next generation, the next generation would be signing up for their college classes while wearing Pampers. (Patience is not one of my virtues.)

Suddenly all I feel for those moms is sympathy. Envy is flushed away. But emotion, like nuclear waste—not the other kind—doesn't disappear even when you flush it. It can poison and contaminate even more effectively when it's hidden.

Look, although I might envy whatever lucky woman is dating George Clooney (living with him in his villa on Lake Como, hearing his wryly insouciant chuckle, running her fingers through his salt-and-pepper hair—oh sorry, are you still here?), that doesn't mean I'm about to abandon my excellent marriage. (After all, we've visited Lake Como, there isn't a day that goes by without something making us laugh together, and I have enough salt-and-pepper hair for two.)

And just because I might envy somebody's review on a newspaper's book page, or their Amazon number, or their attractive author's jacket-flap photograph, that doesn't mean I'm going to stop reading, or going on the computer, or writing. So what if life isn't fair? It's still far more fun than the alternative, according to most reports, and worth making an effort.

12

IF YOU DON'T PAY YOUR EXORCIST,

DO YOU GET REPOSSESSED?

If forty is the new twenty and sixty is the new forty, then is death the new life?

I find that every woman I know becomes increasingly intrigued by the idea of reincarnation as she gets older. We keep thinking of all the things we could have done better. Maybe it's not so much spiritual rebirth that we're looking for as the opportunity for a do-over, as if life were a game of schoolyard kick-ball where you get another chance even if you flub your best shot.

Or maybe we're just experiencing a version of spiritual acid reflux of the essential self, where something that didn't sit right keeps bubbling up to the surface. Forget "Chicken Soup for the Soul": we need "Alka-Selzter for the Soul That Won't Stay Down."

The trouble is that everybody believes she had a really fascinating and exotic past life, whereas I am quite certain that I was toothless, hunchbacked, clubfooted, and no doubt suffered from the heartbreak of psoriasis. I probably also had bad breath and BO; imagine what life was like before Aquafresh and Lady Speed Stick? Everybody smelled like cheese. This is not the stuff you hear about in romance novels. There are rarely passages saying: "With her cat-like eyes of woodland green and her hair as luminous as the finest burnished brass catching the late-afternoon sun, Lady Megan Margaret Lily smelled like a hunk of week-old Jarlsberg if you stood downwind."

I know I wasn't part of Cleopatra's court, that's for sure. Hell, I can't even get into a really good restaurant for lunch. I think most women's past lives, like most women's past husbands, were probably nasty, brutish, and short, but nobody seems to believe that's the case. They all go to psychics and readers to hear about how glorious their previous incarnations were. They want to know that they were Marie Antoinette's handmaiden or Caesar's mistress or Napoléon's favorite serving wench. Basically, they want to picture themselves in low-cut dresses with puffy sleeves and flouncy underskirts. I know I was carrying four kids and a basket of escarole on my back uphill in the one-hundred-degree heat in Calabria somewhere while some bastard named Guillermo was throwing sticks at me from the bottom of the hill because I didn't stuff his sausage correctly.

I have no sense of longing for those days when women were considered "chattel" and people actually knew what the word "chattel" meant; those days are gone. Most of the past is not worth the nostalgia we spend on it. Remember, those ladies didn't have Tampax, they didn't have birth control, and they probably had very few resources when faced with the problem of vaginal dryness.

If anything, you'd think that we would be imagining what our future selves would be like rather than indulging in fantasies of what our past selves were like, but it doesn't work that way, because the past is so much more comforting than the future. It's cozy. It's about goosedown, mead, and really big fireplaces. After all, we know how the story turns out. Plus in the past women were plumper, their hair was wilder, and nobody expected them to pay weekly into their own 401(k)s. They got their advice from Nostradamus, not from Suze Orman; if they needed marital advice, they consulted *The Decameron* as opposed to Dr. Phil.

But remember—and this is one thing we should really remind ourselves about—only six women knew how to read. And I know I wasn't one of them. That's why you won't find me as eager to trace my spiritual genealogy back through the ages as some of my girlfriends, especially the ones who got to inherit furniture made before 1963.

But I do find the idea that some people we have an instant attraction to or an immediate antipathy for are people whom we've encountered in previous existences enthralling. There has to be some reason we're immediately drawn to one particular hot-dog vendor and repelled by another. It can't just be the way they heat up the sauerkraut. I'm perfectly prepared to believe that one of them had been a favorite uncle of mine in a previous life.

I'm also quite prepared to believe that one of the reasons I could never fall in love with one of the guys I dated in college was not because he was too nice but because he had been my brother in some counterpoint lifetime. Even thirty years later, you see, it's hard to believe I could have been so stupid as to have thrown away a really decent relationship to trail after another guy who treated me like landfill just because he had thick, dark hair, a southern drawl, and a really long tongue.

Forces from the occult must have buffeted me about.

That's the only reasonable explanation. And I'm only half-joking. What happens when you realize that you're a plural and not a singular, that the past versions of yourself are still with you?

Half the women you've met have had a series of names. And these are legit women I'm talking about, not the ones who carry Discover Cards in somebody else's name because they find day jobs annoying. I'm talking about regular people—graphic designers, copy editors, teachers, stylists, lawyers, and filmmakers—not ladies who have spent more than one shift at a federal penitentiary.

Women keep renaming ourselves. We have many aliases even when we didn't plan it that way: childhood names, maiden names, married names, professional names, and nicknames.

We make ourselves into nesting dolls and then wonder who's at the center.

So what's the big deal about extending that idea past one little lifetime?

Women have at least one version of ourselves packed away in a suitcase under the bed. She's an escape route. She's another edition, not quite a duplicate, maybe our self from another life. Like the moon, our unknown selves shift and tug at us, exerting forces both profound and unacknowledged. When a feeling washes over us, swells, recedes, carries us off-course, we may not be able to tell where it comes from, but oh, yes, we feel its pull.

No wonder so many of us are convinced this isn't our first life. Personally I've decided that I'm coming back a whole more bunch of times, if only to use all those miniature luxury guest soaps I've brought back from vacations and never dared touch. A later version of me will enjoy them. I've decided to remake my will—I'm going to leave everything to myself.

Our lives are not revealed to us all at once, in whole pieces. Women wipe up, sponge off, take it all in, absorb; we have other people inside of us when we have sex and when we get pregnant— why not at other times? Maybe what some people think of as ghosts are just other selves seeping through in much the same way old patterns bleed through new wallpaper.

Or think about how an elegant tapestry reveals, on its hidden side, a tangled maze of overlapping threads connected in patterns you'd never imagine had you simply looked at the surface.

This is one reason we must be careful of the words we choose; there are other parts of ourselves listening, like children huddled outside a door, drawing their own conclusions.

I started thinking about this because my friend Seri (ironically enough, it's not her real name) is, umm, psychic. I wish there were a less spooky word for it, but there isn't.

Seri picks up indecipherable signals from the bouncing, whirling universe the way a satellite dish picks up TV programs. Actually, her mind is more like an AM radio: lots of static, news, talk, music, scores. The signals may come in, but figuring them out is not her job; the most she'll do is acknowledge them, like nodding to a stranger on the street if there's eye contact.

Seri's peripheral vision has always been crowded, has included a little more than anyone else could see; it was as if she could see print beyond the margins, or read through a sheet of paper to the writing on the back. She knew when the school bus would be late, knew before she got it home when her goldfish would die, knew the names of people she met before she was introduced to them.

Having no suitable vocabulary, grammar, or syntax with which to make a coherent story of her odd experiences as a child, she started calling them by the name her mother used: woo-woo.

It's a term I adore.

Only a few of her friends know about Seri's "woo-woo."

That's because we all tease her, demanding, "C'mon, Seri: just tell us what stocks to buy." Or, slightly more seriously, we ask about medications ("Is this stuff going to be pulled from the market in five years for killing people?" "Am I going to become addicted to Ambien if I start taking it?") or if buying a new car is worth the bother ("Will the old Volvo keep me rolling along?" "Would I be wiser to lease a hybrid car even though I wouldn't feel quite as safe?").

But Seri decided when she was very young that, although she might not know exactly what "woo-woo" was, she knew enough not to fool with it. Or, at least, not to invite it to cross her threshold. The few times in the past when she's done that have not provided her with the happiest of memories. She attempts to repress the "woo-woo," but it's still there, like an old friend you can't ditch once you become popular.

Seri gets signals; she picks up all kinds of information about her clients at the salon where she works as a nail tech, as if sneaking into the back of a darkened room to watch their home movies. But even as she sees their inner lives unfold in front of her the minute she takes their hand in her own, she never lets on. That's not what they pay a nail technician for. They come for a French fill. "This woo-woo thing," Seri says, "is like getting phone calls from people you don't want to talk to when you're desperate to hear from somebody else."

Sometimes Seri gets what she calls "the spooks" when the rosy world turns gray at the edges and people communicate things to her she would rather not hear. But it seldom goes on for more than an hour or two; she tells people she has a headache and goes to bed and sings "Hold My Hand" by Hootie and the Blowfish louder and louder until "the spooks" give up and go away. It has nothing to do with the aesthetics of the song; it's just that she can carry that particular tune.

If you poke your finger through into the other world, you make a hole, and it can return the privilege. Is it a surprise, really? If you can crash the sound barrier, why not the time barrier? Plow through it like a Hummer through a backyard fence?

Look, I'm not suggesting that we spend our lives like somebody sitting facing backward in a train, always looking at what's already passed, or that we all hold "come as you were" parties on anything but Halloween.

Yet I suspect that time is not locked into the security of the past tense as we've been taught to believe. I suspect, too, that it may be possible to waltz almost effortlessly onto the dance floor of the supernatural if we'd only let ourselves hear the beat.

Even if that beat is to a song by Hootie and the Blowfish.

13

WHERE ARE THE OUIJA WOMEN

WHEN YOU NEED THEM?

I've been thinking a lot about psychic activity. But then you already knew that.

When driving through a rather bleak town in Northern California, my husband noticed a sign reading: Psychic Fair This Weekend. "Wouldn't you like to go?" he asked me, knowing of my deep, if embarrassing, fascination for the subject. "But it doesn't give any information about where or when," I point out. Slyly, he replied, "If you have to ask, you don't belong there."

My interest in psychics, in reincarnation, in ghosts, in past lives, in dreams, and in other things unnerving has always been my secret vice. I buy books on the paranormal the way other people buy pornography. I ask that they be sent in plain brown wrappers with no identifying feature visible to anyone's prying eyes.

Only if somebody can tell what's in the parcel through the brown paper wrapper is he or she welcome to start a conversation.

But I don't want to keep it to myself anymore. I've decided to stop sneaking around. I've decided that an interest in the topic doesn't mean I'm going to start saying, "I see dead people." After all, that phrase only really applied when I was dating.

No doubt a lot of this emerged from the primordial ooze of my combined Sicilian/French-Canadian heritage. We were not so much Christians as we were pagans with a light coating of Roman Catholicism. My aunts who all wore black lace mantillas would go to church to yell at God and light candles. They also lit candles at home. We're not talking some kind of scented housewarming candles. They weren't doing this for feng shui. They were doing this so that the disgruntled dead would be less likely to wreak havoc on their lives. There was a belief somehow that the dead obviously didn't have enough to do. We knew for example that there was no sex in heaven, but that wouldn't have taken up so much time anyhow. But it became clear that there probably weren't any card games in heaven, either. No pinochle, gin rummy, or even Po•Ke•No (those who know will know). So the dead had a lot of time on their hands, obviously. Which meant that they liked to come and interfere. "It's your aunt Josie who moves everything," my grandmother would say when I couldn't find a pen that I'd put down. She shuffles things around when she thinks we're not paying enough attention to her. "If you can't find something, even when you know where you've put it, just say, 'Aunt Josie, come on, let me find my pen please,' and leave the room for a couple of minutes.

When you come back, the odds are ten to one that you'll find the pen just where you thought you'd already looked."

You might need to deal with a fancier dead person if things were more complicated. If Aunt Josie couldn't help you find what you were looking for, you might need to apply to Saint Anthony, the Finder of Lost Objects. Apparently Saint Anthony liked when you took two chairs and tied them together back-to-back in the middle of the room. If you did that, you could virtually guarantee finding whatever was lost. "The only thing it doesn't work for is virginity," snickered my cousin Marie.

I always thought that my interest in strange stuff had to do with the mostly all-female world in which I was raised. Both official and unofficial spiritual lives seemed the provenance of women. Men didn't bother much with any of this (except for my one gay uncle, who seemed as interested in the whole business as any of his sisters). I learned that my father was not immune to magic, its threats or its promises, when on my twelfth birthday a friend gave me a Ouija board. My friends and I were all in the basement of the house my family had recently moved into on Long Island. There were probably six of us girls. All giggling and smudging up against each other in the dark while our fingertips rolled the little wheelie thing around the board.

Suddenly Bonnie screamed. "I felt something! I really felt something!" she yelled. I hurried to switch on the light. The room felt cold and it took only the flicker of a second to realize that we were all genuinely scared. My father ran down the stairs, asking what the hell had happened, and started to laugh when we told him what we were doing. "For a bunch of smart girls, you're all morons," declared my father as he ushered us up the stairs for soda and cake in the sunny afternoon.

Only two years ago, and only after plying my aged father with two of my husband's significantly potent martinis, did I discover that my father was genuinely worried by the incident in the basement. He explained that the only reason he got to buy the house as cheaply as he did was because the family who'd originally owned the house had planned to give it to their son on his wedding and this son died the night before the wedding was to have taken place. "They just wanted to get rid of the place. They had even left all his things in the attic. His games, his books, his uniform from Korea. All that was still there when we moved in and I thought it would be bad luck to touch it."

"You mean, we lived with that guy's stuff in the house the whole time we were there?" I had never been up to the attic—there was no staircase and as far as I knew no reason to go up there.

"What can I tell you?" sipped my father. "I just didn't see any reason for your friends to get in touch with this guy, inviting him to come back and claim the house as his."

My father admitted, too, that directly after shooing us into the kitchen he went down to the basement and put salt in the corners of the room in order to drive out any spirits that might have lingered.

We were not a particularly sophisticated bunch. My interest in the spooky went underground during college, although when my roommate and I would go study in the graveyard during the summer term—it was the prettiest place on campus—we always made sure to say hello to the guys on whose ghostly laps we were sitting.

And, of course like many other people, I've also had romantic rendezvous in cemeteries. Oh, admit it—you have, too. Haven't you ever walked away only to find your T-shirt emblazoned with a grave rubbing of "He Is Risen"?

But studying and fooling around seemed to me to be things of which the dead would approve. Only now in the middle of my middle age can I admit that my interest is still vital. When I dream about the dead, it does feel as if I'm getting some kind of digitally transmitted picture the way someone would send you vacation pictures as an e-mail attachment.

My adoring husband, who sums up my interest in these matters as "nuts," gave me a fabulous birthday present where he rented a limo and had six of my friends and me taken to see a psychic in another state (not because he was afraid that someone in-state would recognize us but because this guy had a good reputation, and I am saying that without irony). When one of us was getting a reading the rest of us were getting our nails done at a salon next door. Then we all went to eat and discussed our past and future lives.

To be honest, the conversation was probably pretty much what it would have been had we not gone to see the psychic—the past and the future being the subjects of our usual conversation on any evening when we all got together and launched ourselves into food and wine.

Maybe part of what attracts me to these ideas is that they take us to places that are already familiar: they ask us questions about who we have been and who we are going to be.

Finally, I'll admit that although there are gender-specific activities in life, we can often find connections between them. In this case, the connections are easy to make. A man goes to a strip club for the same reason a woman goes to a psychic: to have something revealed.

14

WHAT DO YOU MEAN,

"LOSE WEIGHT *FATS*"?

"*I sincerely apologize* if you are receiving this e-mail in error," said one of the many messages I opened this morning. I usually delete the generic e-mails, the ones that are not actually addressed to me, first thing, even before I have a cup of coffee. This is because I do not want or need to be conscious to deal with them. Heavy-lidded and yawning, I push the "trash" button automatically while the fog in my brain begins to clear.

For some reason (Too little sleep? Distracted by the cats that have decided to sink their tiny fangs into my ankles?), I make a horrible error and *open* one of these missives. Confronting my practically somnolent self is the following message: "I have saved my family and my life. Because of this I have made a commitment to get the word out on this life-changing product, so that it will be available to everyone."

The words sank into my consciousness despite all desire to block them out. I can't blame my easily won attention simply on the lack of caffeine or the inability to avert my eyes once I start reading; I can't even blame it on the same prurient kind of curiosity that makes me read *Weekly World News* while waiting on the grocery line. At least that's *fun* and the only folks who truly believe what's printed are ones who have nurtured Bat Boys in their own respective belfries.

What hooked my attention in the unsolicited mail was the use of the pathetically personal introductory material, as quoted here directly: "My name is Dana Hampton. I'm a married 37-year-old mother of 4 who was a happy size 7 before my first child and who grew 4 dress sizes larger by my fourth pregnancy. I didn't like the way I looked and I didn't like the way I felt. . . . Just didn't want to live and have to face another day."

Boy, can't you just see her? Wearing too-tight jeans and a sparkly top, hair lank around her pudding face, gaudy earrings and bracelets dangling in order to detract from her contours ("draw the eye upward!"), and surrounded by pale, round, gooey-eyed children circling her like mushrooms? Her house is always sticky and a television buzzes in the background like flies. She is on the very verge of despair, dreams of youth and beauty gone, weeps at commercials for dog food and long-distance carriers, and spends her time remembering when life was good as a "size 7"?

So what did she need? A supportive community? A good foun-

dation garment? Counseling? A checkup with her physician? Birth
control? A job to get her out of the house and into a world where
her skills and intelligence could be validated? Exercise? Adequate
child care? Renewal of her spiritual life? A marriage-encounter
weekend? Fewer Little Debbie cupcakes?

Turns out all she needed to go from stuffed duck to swinging
swan was a few pills she got off the Internet.

I kept reading. God help me, I kept reading, picturing this lady
and hoping that she did *indeed* find happiness through the use of
non-FDA-approved vitamin supplements. Having invested this
much energy, I wanted to read the happy ending in a hurry.

"The greatest compliment I got was from my husband," she explains. "He told me that I 'looked younger.' He said my face looked
especially younger, 'you look like the real you!' "

Naturally by this point I am cheering along, relieved at the
sense of love brought back from the brink, as well as of a life re-
gained and made whole. "Recently," she continues, building to
the finale, "he told me, 'Olivia, you really look great, you look like
the young girl I kissed at our wedding.' "

The next line of type—I'm not changing anything and I certainly could never have made this up—is as follows: "I said,
'What?' "

I'd be saying, "What?" too. Wouldn't you? Not because her
husband has rediscovered he loves his wife because of her dress
size, nor would I suggest that saying "you look like the young girl
I kissed at our wedding" could easily imply the husband was pulling
a Sonny Corleone (and kissing a young girl who was not necessarily

even related to his bride at his wedding), but because the name given by the woman at the beginning of the e-mail, as you remember, is "Dana."

Who the hell is Olivia?

If you can't trust people revealing their life stories in order to sell you tacky weight-loss drugs, who *can* you trust?

The lesson? No reading before the first cup of coffee.

15

WHAT I WISH I'D KNOWN SOONER

It's a shock, but I've learned that many of the truths conferred upon me—by poets, mentors, and needlepointed pillows available in the clearance area of major discount home-goods stores—are deliberate falsehoods.

Can you believe it?

You know those instructions you've pored over, supplied by Ikea or Pottery Barn or Apple, reassuring you that they provide "tips" for "easy assembly"? How they said if you just press this, hit that, juxtapose that with this, and then wait a few moments, you will have the key to all happiness in the palm of your hot little hand? You know how those flimsy pieces of paper give you what you believe is good advice that turns out to be entirely false, causing you to yell and throw things?

Well, maybe cosmic and cultural instruction sheets function in a manner quite similar to the flimsy pieces of paper, literal and metaphorical, we attempt to use as currency in our emotional lives.

As a starting point, let's begin with the idea that a person should not believe everything a person reads, even when it is said beautifully, seductively, and with supreme authority.

Which means the first item we need to disassemble is the concept that, as Shakespeare put it in Sonnet 116: "Love is not love / Which alters when it alteration finds."

Sure it is.

Of course love is subject to change. Like a good wine or bad haircuts, love alters over time. And sometimes, too, it goes away. Which does not mean it wasn't there in the first place.

Love changes, shifts, swerves into other lanes, changes its name, address, phone number, and favorite color. And, as with wine or haircuts, you can—at some point and for any number of reasons—stop loving what you once adored.

Next point: "Grow where you are planted." This applies only to vegetable matter. What are you, an endive? Get out of your little patch of dirt and do something.

Not everything gets better with time. For example, people who dislike you instantly will not come to like you better as time passes. You will not correct their opinion. The smart money is that they will like you less. Stop trying to please them.

"Everything you need to know you learned in kindergarten." I guess we should stop wondering why Johnny can't read and why the federal government can't do math.

Remember, please, that the first time you make yourself miserable over some profound misstep, your friends will find it—and your despair—tragic. By the nineteenth time you make yourself miserable over the same category of heartbreak, however, be assured that even your most sympathetic friends are regarding the event as a farce. This applies to choosing the wrong job, wrong apartment, wrong partner, and SSRI, as well as binge-eating, two-day benders, four-hour tirades concerning how your parents pushed you into their idea of success while never nurturing your real talents, and contacting old lovers by e-mail in the middle of the night. Just stop it.

How about "diamonds are a girl's best friends"? Nope. It should be switched around and pointed out, instead, that your best friends are diamonds. (Even Anita Loos knew this.) It's your best friends who are supremely resilient, everlasting, made under pressure, and of astonishing value. Also, there is no such thing as "fake diamonds" just as there are no such things as "false friends." Either they are or they aren't. Imitations are tacky, easily spotted, and likely to fall off if you expose them to hot water.

"Handsome is as handsome does"? Sorry. Cute is cute. Stop kidding yourself.

"Love is blind." No, love is not blind. See above. But love is certainly hard of hearing. If people always heard what other people said, or did not choose to ignore what they meant, it would be impossible to be in love.

"You don't have to pet to be popular"? If you want to be really popular, yes, you do.

Finally, there is a celebrated aphorism insisting that the best way to live is to "work like you don't need the money, dance like nobody is watching, and love like you've never been hurt." Lots of otherwise sensible individuals have gone all mushy reading those lines. Some of them have been driven to have the lines inscribed on pieces of jewelry, placed at the end of their e-mails, or tattooed on their necks.

After years of hearing and reading these lines I have decided to tell the truth: *the original version is wrong*. There is a grave error in the wording of this adage.

The correct version should go as follows:

Love like you don't need the money,
Work like nobody is watching,
Dance like you've never been hurt.

See? Doesn't that make more sense?

16

WHY DO I MAKE MYSELF MISERABLE FOR PAYING ANOTHER WOMAN TO CLEAN MY HOUSE?

I was prompted to write about the importance of housekeeping when I read a news report, coming out of Italy, with the following title: "Woman Kidnapped by Ex-Partner to Clean Home." According to a police report, an Italian man was arrested on suspicion of kidnapping his ex-girlfriend from a pub and "forcing her to iron his clothes and wash the dishes at his home." The forty-three-year-old man "dragged the woman out of a pub in the port city of Genoa, shoved her into a car and took her to his home, where he made her do his household chores after threatening her."

It took arrest and the specter of prison to make this man feel that he'd done something wrong in forcing another human being to clean his house. So why do I feel bad paying someone to do it?

I feel guilty about having another woman clean my house, but not guilty enough to do it myself.

"Tell them I get paid for it," Heidi instructs, reading over my shoulder. "This is not an act of love. It's my job. Now lift up your feet. And stop analyzing everything already. Okay, you can put your feet back."

I'm trying to get rid of guilt; my goal is to replace it with humility and gratitude. I'm trying especially hard to distinguish between genuine humility and its evil twin, humiliation.

Not so easy.

Humiliation is when you're worried that others will see your inadequacies ("I'm embarrassed to be seen without mascara because I look like a mole only with smaller eyes"; "I'm horrified that if my kids are dumb or spoiled, people will think I'm a bad mother"; "I hate driving a gas-guzzler—I feel like everybody thinks I paid no attention to Earth Day").

Humility is when you think not about how you will be judged by others but about how you can help them—or even how you can think about them ("Nobody looks at me on the beach now that they're all watching my live ferret—I can just enjoy myself with my friends and splash around"; "If my kids are clean and happy, I'm doing a great job"; "I'm giving my neighbor a lift to the hospital—he doesn't care what year my car was made").

The big difference is that humiliation is about yourself and humility is about realizing that you are not all that important in the grand scheme of things—except when you can make a difference.

And that can be a big relief.

Let's go back to feeling rotten about the fact that I am not the queen of clean. There are a number of reasons for this. I am a not a great cleaner, even though I know how to do it. As a teenager, I cleaned houses as a part-time job. I was cleaning somebody else's house the afternoon my mother died, the summer I was sixteen, got the phone call, and felt bad about leaving the job only half-done. This was entirely self-imposed. The lady whose kitchen floor I was washing did not scowl at me in a Dickensian manner or anything. She was sympathetic and kind. I made myself feel bad—nobody did it to me.

I felt terrible, of course, about my mother's illness and death. Not that there was anything I could do about it—cancer teaches a fast and hard course in humility. But I was haunted by the thought that maybe I could have been a better daughter, been more attentive, less argumentative, more loving. Actually, I was a pretty good kid. Probably because I had a pretty good mother. I began to forgive myself for being incapable of saving her when I began to forgive my mother for being incapable of saving herself. Which took, by the way, years of therapy; this wasn't a sudden flash of insight that came from watching a daytime TV show or reading a self-help book.

Yet I had, early on in life, developed a taste for guilt. I apologized for rainy days or if I got stuck in traffic. I apologized for having a name with a lot of vowels, difficult to spell if I was ordering a gift from a catalog.

I apologized for being single, for being unhappily married, for being divorced, for being a second wife, for being a stepmother, for being happily married.

I apologized for not having my old relatives live with me (too little); I apologized for speaking to my father every day (too much).

In graduate school, I apologized for not having a "real" job; when I got a "real" job, I apologized for having one.

I couldn't let myself win. If I did, then I would have to accept the enormous responsibility of continuing to live up to that moment as well as the obligation of helping other folks do as well.

It sounded pretty tiring. Guilt is easier than action.

My apologies did exactly this much good for anybody else: my guilt did even less good since it hurt me and sucked up energy I could have used for kindness, or generosity, or hard work, which might have genuinely helped someone else.

Not that I have it all figured out. When I mess up, I still feel bad about my mistakes. I then try to admit them instantly, rectify them quickly, and understand them as soon as possible in order not to repeat them. It is hard and does not always work.

But it is better than guilt.

17

WOULD SATAN FLOSS?

Why are bad habits easier to adopt than good ones? I'm not even talking about interesting bad habits, like having unsafe sex with strangers or drinking until you don't remember your age. I'm talking about things such as flossing.

Flossing: that was the example bringing the topic to mind (and mouth). Other people don't have trouble flossing their teeth; they just floss away, morning, noon, and night—veritable flossing fools—never even thinking about those of us who wish to floss, indeed long to floss, but find ourselves unable to get into the habit.

We, the floss forgotten, carry sample floss with us, hoping to catch ourselves at a vulnerable, open moment when new, good habits can emerge. We envy those who floss easily, even if we hide our envy for fear of ridicule or recrimination.

It's a simple thing, flossing one's teeth (flossing the teeth of others is no doubt much more complicated and should be the subject of another chapter). Yet I seem to be constitutionally incapable of forcing myself into this indisputably good habit.

I have no problem, in contrast, picking up bad habits on contact, as if vice were a kind of moral lint that just attaches itself to me at every occasion. Bad habits, however, cannot be removed with a simple flick of the brush. If I avoid vice (and that little word "if" is not merely rhetorical in this context), it is only because wickedness tempts me to the bone. If I make sane choices, they are chosen only because the unavoidable insanity of the tempting options is clear even behind their veil of seduction.

If I go to the casino, which I do maybe four times a year at most, I can imagine all too easily sitting at a slot machine for the rest of my natural life, throwing away quarters as if good fortune were always twenty-five cents away. If I smoke a cigarette, something I do even more rarely than I go to the casino, I can far too easily picture myself becoming a committed, avid, lifelong (and that life wouldn't last very long) chain-smoker.

In contrast, good habits always seem tougher to bring on board: the image of hauling them up from the sea of virtue like iron weights (iron is good for you, right?) is a daunting one.

Another example? Fiber, like flossing, is reported to be a good habit. I guess you are meant to *eat* fiber, but for all I know, you're supposed to floss with it. (I don't suppose we could all just chomp on dental floss once a day, count it as fiber, and get the whole business over with, do you?) I like broccoli and cauliflower as much as the next person, but I prefer brownies and ice cream. If

I manage to eat broccoli and cauliflower, I want them to be smothered in a rich cheese sauce, which no doubt irrevocably prevents goodness from their fiber being channeled into my cheese-ridden system. Let's say that the cheese in the recipe trumps the fiber.

The trouble is, the vices of others are difficult to understand. There is, for instance, the excellent habit of actually meeting your deadlines. I quite like deadlines, because they force me to sit down and do my job. Other people I know and love, however, can no more be expected to meet a deadline than they could look at their own tombstone with aplomb. For certain types, after all, "deadline" and "death" are practically synonymous. It is hard for me to comprehend that, for some people, "deadline" is as terrifying a term as "fiber" and "floss" combined. A certain man I know very well (name supplied upon request) has constructed a sort of cozy tradition around not quite getting his work completed on time. Does it bother him? Yes. Does it bother him enough to change his ways? No.

Therein lies the catch. If my teeth were falling out like Chiclets, I'd do my dental duty without hesitation. If the man described above actually forfeited one single molecule of self-esteem, stature, respect, or work because of his habitual procrastination, he would alter his wicked ways instantaneously.

But my smile and his reputation for unmatched excellence remain intact.

As I write, however, I see warning flares shoot up on the horizon: Embrace flossing. Meet deadlines.

Yet I've also learned that all the unreservedly good habits in the world don't make for a good person: real villains sometimes floss their teeth (you can smile and smile and be a villain); true scoundrels often eschew rescheduling.

Of course good habits and good people do occasionally go together. But remember: goodness takes practice; it is more than just a habit.

18

WHY DO I FEEL PITY FOR

MY CLOTHES?

When I was attempting to explain the pervasive nature of my guilt to a friend, I offered as evidence that I feel guilty when certain clothes fall out of circulation.

"Of course you feel guilty about your clothes. Every woman feels guilty about her clothes," she said dismissively.

"I don't mean that I feel guilty that I've spent money on them and they're just hanging there. That would be logical. That might actually make sense," I explained. "What I meant is that I am deeply concerned about the emotional response my garments might have when they are no longer worn on a regular basis."

"You mean, like you might have a paisley jacket from 1994 that grieves silently because it no longer goes out on the weekend? Are you worried that a pair of red shoes with heels too high to be worn without an oxygen mask might weep when you're not look-ing? Do you have lingerie so wounded by a lack of attention that it might consider getting together with your old slips and filing a class action suit against you for neglect?"

"Sort of."

"Sweetie," she sighed, "you might be alone in this one."

I don't think I am. If I'm all nerdy and anxious about some-thing, my bet has always been that I could find other women just as nerdy and anxious as I am.

It didn't take long for me to find excellent company. Karen understood the concept immediately, even though she doesn't, herself, focus on clothing as a means of self-flagellation.

"You mean like when you line your stuffed animals up and leave them there for a while, but you discover you need to arrange them every so often, so that the ones you like best aren't always in the privileged position, because that might make the green elephant your aunt gave you feel bad since you never really liked him? So you occasionally put your green elephant at the head of the line in order to disguise your true feelings for him? I understand that entirely."

Melissa also understood the concept and could, indeed, relate it to clothing and accessories.

"When I clean out my closet, I have to channel this evil step-mother persona because I feel so bad about getting rid of these clothes I've hoarded for years. It's like putting orphans out in the snow. But, seriously, when am I ever going to wear a sunflower print empire-waist dress post-2002?"

I ask her whether the wearing is the point or is it instead severing the emotional involvement with the dress that's at the heart of this?

"Maybe we invest these clothes with all this energy because we wore them during some particularly meaningful moment in our own lives? I can just imagine the sunflower dress pleading with me not to let it rot away at the Salvation Army or go into the arms of some stranger off the street, because it saw me through my first kiss."

Karen's boyfriend weighed in with, "I have three suits I bought when I was still working in the corporate world. They still have the tags on them. Does that count?"

"No!" we all shouted in unison. "You don't feel guilty about not wearing those clothes. You just feel stupid because you paid money for them. It's entirely different."

I was adamant about the point. If I haven't worn something for more than two years, I find a good home for the skirt or the jacket. Unfortunately, unlike stray animals, you can't really neuter your clothing. I, for one, keep wanting to find the perfect pair of black pants even though I have maybe fourteen pairs of black pants already.

I know I should just wear these. I know that when my husband says that I do not "need" another pair of black pants he is not attempting to repress my need for self-expression. I know that he simply cannot understand why I would add to an already-crowded closet an item that looks—to his untutored gaze—exactly like everything else I own.

Maybe I'm just trying to make up for those years when I was a kid, when I had a brown skirt and top, a blue skirt and top, and a pink party dress and that's it. I had a pair of school shoes and a pair of sneakers. On my seventh birthday, I asked for a headband with fake flowers stuck to it, but my uncle Bill said to my mother, "Anne, make her take that thing off. She looks like a farmer," a phrase that prevented me from accessorizing for many years. I'm not getting out the violins here—I wasn't exactly the Little Match Girl dressed in rags—but because of these early experiences I do feel simultaneously entitled to and guilty about the pleasures of clothing. Maybe it's because what I really wish is that I could take my twelve-year-old self shopping.

19

WHY, OH WHY,

DID I WATCH *NO COUNTRY FOR OLD MEN*

AFTER SHOPPING AT ANN TAYLOR?

Maybe it was a mistake to see the adaptation of Cormac Mc-Carthy's *No Country for Old Men* at the mall multiplex last weekend. I'm not upset that the screen was no bigger than my microwave; I've discovered that my students watch entire films on their iPod Nanos and somehow find it amusing. No, I have larger philosophical issues to weigh in on—or simply to weigh.

The problem, you see, came from watching a decidedly guy movie after undergoing some undeniably girly shopping at Ann Taylor, J. Jill, and Victoria's Secret. The juxtaposition of these gender-specific activities was perhaps disorienting, and it made me wonder what Mr. McCarthy (and the Coen brothers, for that matter) would do if their protagonists, instead of being a soul-searching sheriff, a conscience-burdened psychopath, and a stunningly naïve fugitive thief, had been my fellow Christmas shoppers and myself: vaguely middle-aged ladies, overworked, overanxious, and overfed.

The result would still have to be, of course, pure McCarthy. Spare, violent, clipped.

Contest with fate. Moments of the irrevocable.

Self-awareness at a cost, but what cost?

And could you have found it wholesale?

It might go something like this:

The "20% off" signs shimmered on the polished quiet of the sales floor. A brightly lit world. No visible shadows, not with them new halogen overheads. The big woman, dressed in black except for one lone flower pinned to her lapel, stood next to the register with her manicured hands crossed in front of her.

These are her thoughts.

There would be nails broke by the end of the day. For what? Nothing. For a holiday rush, for women buying stuff they didn't need for folks who didn't want it. Yeah. Well. Everybody gets what they deserve at this time of year. Retail ain't no place for sissies. She breathed her last deep breath; then the bells rang. Them front doors opened and the stampede started.

I don't know if retail work is more upsetting now than what it used to be or not. I know when I first starting selling women's separates, you'd have a bad time somewheres near the sale counters during the holiday season and you'd go to break it up and they'd offer to fight you. And sometimes you had to accommodate 'em. They wouldn't have it no other way. And you'd better not lose, neither. You don't see that so much no more, but maybe you see worse. I had a woman pull a cell phone on me one time to contact the corporate headquarters and it happened that I grabbed it just as she went to fire off a text message and the charm on her bracelet left a mark on the fleshy part of my thumb. You can see the imprint of Minnie Mouse right there.

I sent one gal to the dressing room with a size M when I knew for dead certain she was an L. Maybe even an XL. I sure didn't want to. She wasn't no more than thirty-five years old, neither. She deserved better. But I couldn't make myself say the raw truth. Not in front of all those itty-bitty ladies, some XPs even, who was glancing at her sideways like, snickering under their breath and wondering why she was holding Dolce & Gabbana pants when she was packing those thighs under that wide, vast landscape of a waist.

That thirty-five-year-old lady, well, she told me that she had been planning to meet her high-school sweetheart for lunch. Said she would wear these here Italian slacks. Told me out of her own mouth. Didn't stutter a bit. Not like my idiot assistant Thelma who don't know how to say "Dolce and Gabbana" without making them sound like one of them Ben & Jerry ice-cream flavors.

I thought I'd never seen a person like that lady, not in

twelve years of working retail, and it got me to wonderin' if maybe she was some new kind. A fat woman who didn't know she was fat.

What about me? I started wonderin'. Was I one of her kin without knowin' it? I looked down at these thighs of my own, the ones I been sportin' since I was a girl.

They say for a woman that the thighs are the windows to the soul.

I don't know what them thighs on that lady was the windows to and I guess I'd as soon not know. Wondering has done brought me to a place in my life I would not of thought I'd come to.

And that place ain't anywhere near Hollywood or the bestseller list of *The New York Times*. It ain't even near the ladies' room, which is up on the fourth floor. Damn.

(Next time I'll shop *after* going to the movies.)

20

HOW MUCH OF A CRAZY

ASTRONAUT LADY ARE YOU?

You can divide women into two groups: ones who understand the crazy astronaut lady and ones who don't.

You remember the CAL, right? A pretty brunette who tried to hunt down her rival, aka Lisa Nowak, née Caputo. I include her maiden name for one reason: discovering she was of Italian extraction made me instantly at one with her. To adapt Flaubert's line, the crazy astronaut lady: *è* me.

Nowak became famous on February 5, 2007, when she was arrested in Orlando, Florida, for attempting to kidnap the girlfriend of her former lover, astronaut William Oefelein.

Hey, when you're trained by NASA, you're good at making plans; when you're consumed by jealousy and competitive lust, however, you might find it a little tricky to carry them out.

Lisa Nowak drove from Texas to Florida without stopping. She was Thelma without Louise but with less liquor, no Brad Pitt, even more anger.

My deeply complex and thoroughly researched theory concerning a sociological division of women into two groups is based on the following: I've heard that there are women who simply don't understand how a sober, otherwise industrious individual could suddenly pack latex gloves, a black wig, a BB pistol, pepper spray, black gloves, a tan trench coat with a hood, a hammer drill, rubber tubing, Glad bags, about $585 cash, her laptop, an eight-inch Gerber folding knife, and adult diapers, drive nine hundred miles, and confront her lover's new girlfriend in an airport parking lot.

And the rest of us understand that entirely.

Not only do we understand that entirely, but we spend time thinking about what else she might have packed in order to make the escapade more successful. (Why the black wig? She was already a brunette. Why not go blond?)

We're the ones who have the crazy astronaut lady within. We understand because most of us have had at least one relationship that made us crazy. The force of certain relationships causes us to go gothically, awesomely insane. The blast from these emotionally climactic moments rips apart the infrastructure of our lives so completely that the only things left are the cockroach feelings: the most basic, meanest, blindly driven, indestructible parts of the self that come out only in the dark.

And though there might be howls of outrage, I'm going to say

it: life is richer if you've had to deal with one of these relationships. To love and not to be loved in return is the ultimate hum-
bling experience.

Even more terrifying is to have been loved profoundly once
and to be loved no longer.

It makes you a lot less snotty.

It makes you a lot less likely to say things such as, "But why
doesn't she just leave him if she's so unhappy . . . ?" or "Where
is her self-respect?" or "I'd never let anybody treat me like
that."

I'm not talking about the kind of people who make themselves
miserable habitually; I have no patience for self-indulgence as a
form of self-discipline. I can't abide people who plunge themselves into the psychological abyss as a hobby, the way that other
people might go spelunking. I'm easily bored by people who are
always in a relationship that nearly kills them and who regard this
as evidence for the appetite for life.

I'm talking about those singular relationships where, despite
yourself, you're willing to sacrifice good sense on the altar of pas-
sion.

I spent a certain amount of time making myself and everyone
around me crazy; that period of life lasted from approximately
1974 to 1998.

It was like my entire emotional life was a piñata and I was
walking around underneath it, blindfolded and with a bat. I would
be swinging the bat wildly into the air, having, of course, no idea
what I was doing because I was wearing a blindfold, swinging at

the piñata, and screaming, "Aieeeeee!" while saner people ran away.

They were running away from me, because I was a screaming blindfolded lady with a bat. Who could blame them? If I could have slammed the door on myself, I certainly would have done as much.

I was a version of the astronaut lady but afraid of heights and less toned.

I, of course, assumed that the people around me simply didn't love me enough—I believed, according to multiple journal entries, they were "just people who couldn't love," who, with my characteristic lack of judgment, I kept choosing to be my life's companions.

I scribbled endlessly about how they would abandon me when these perfectly logical moments of true misery, depression, anger, and anarchy overwhelmed me, as they just happened to do on a schedule so regular that Nowak's colleagues at NASA could have used it to chart their satellites.

I worried about loving the people around me "too much." Now I realize that the concept is absurd. It's impossible to love somebody too much. What you can do, and what I did, was behave like a moron, using my "great love" as a excuse to behave selfishly and act badly, damaging myself and wrecking those around me, sweeping through certain periods of life like a tornado through an emotional trailer park.

It wasn't pretty.

It's never pretty to live with the fear of being abandoned, because if you're abandoned, you're left behind; you're emptied out. Right? You're like an abandoned building, vacated, ripe for the next tenant.

Hmm. Maybe that isn't so bad. Maybe you don't have to rent out; maybe you can own the whole structure and have an occasional visitor—without having a renter or offering anybody a lease.

Maybe being a woman *of* abandon is something else. Maybe that's the kind of abandon to embrace, the kind that announces unapologetically, "I'm making the decisions here, I don't care. I'm not paying attention anymore to all that shit you told me, all those rules, all those ways you're telling me I'm supposed to stay stable and good."

A woman of abandon is somebody stripping off all the ties that bind her down.

Somebody who does something *with* abandon: now, that's almost the same, but it has to do with something positive, not negative, not just the throwing away of restraint but the embrace of appetite.

The embrace of appetite, like the reassurance of abundance, depends on the idea that there *is* enough.

So what are the lessons here, the ones our poor sister CAL never learned? I suggest that these five points might help us guide ourselves: 1. Let loose with your affections, but don't waste them on a loser; 2. If you feel like you're "too much" for a guy to handle, weigh carefully the possibility that he's simply not enough for you; 3. If you cry more than three times per week on a regular basis, do not consider this romantic, interesting, or feminine—see it as a sign that you need to get more sleep, a different live-in companion, a new job, and/or, if these don't help, some serious time with a counselor; 4. Never make the long drive from Texas to Florida, especially if you are trained and licensed to fly space-ships; 5. Remember that "Crazy" is a great Patsy Cline song, but it is decidedly not the word you want inscribed on your tombstone.

21

"WILL THIS SHROUD MAKE ME

LOOK FAT?"

*f*or *years now* we've been hearing, as if the phrase contained great wisdom: "Nobody on his deathbed ever said, 'I wish I'd spent more time in the office.'"

This is supposed to remind us to enjoy every day and not work too hard. Yeah, like that's a really big problem for most people. Maybe for some folks that little sanctimonious phrase has played the terribly important role of permitting them to spend even more time in the employees' restroom when they're supposed to be do-ing their job, but all it does for me is make me wonder about the person on his or her deathbed.

Maybe if he stayed at work, he wouldn't have contracted Saint Vitus' dance? Maybe if she'd spent more time at the office, she'd have developed a formula to prevent or a way to cure what's ailing her? "Hey, girls, c'mon over here! Celia just found the cure for Everything! Thank goodness she didn't try traveling off-peak!"

There are worse things to do than work. If you really hate your job, sure, it's a drag. And rotten jobs are easy to come by. Just watch an episode of *Who Wants to Be a Millionaire?* and you'll see just how eager most people are to stop pulling down a paycheck. They'll risk any humiliation for a long shot at the chance; the same thing goes for being put on the ticket as a candidate for the vice presidency. ("Look, honey! We don't have to worry about retire-ment or health care anymore! Everybody else in the country does, sure, but not us!")

But this well-worn phrase specifies "office" and so implies a fancy job, one of those professions where *you* get to decide how long you work—not a place where somebody else tells you to punch in and out.

The thought that a person's biggest regret is having spent too much time doing his or her work in life means that the person un-der discussion here has not found the right kind of labor. And I'm not just saying that because I'm a teacher and teaching is a good job with benefits and because teaching is a worthy vocation, blah-blahblah (although of course it is and I am grateful). I know some people actually like to work, however, because of the people I grew up with.

My father, for example, who sold window treatments until he was eighty-one and the Parkinson's took over, liked his job even more than I like mine, and that's saying something. Selling stuff to people in Manhattan wasn't the easiest job, either. One of his prized possessions was a sweatshirt declaring: "You can't scare me. I'm in retail." (Somehow I don't think you could sell as many sweatshirts saying: "You can't scare me. I'm in higher education.")

So if you don't think about work as a waste of time—and since I don't, I bet you don't, either—then what *is* a waste of time?

I started wondering what might be the last thoughts on having misspent one's time in life. I started thinking about what Saint Peter at the Pearly Gates might deduct points for having spent lots of time doing when you might have been doing something useful (like having a conversation with a friend, or eating, or laughing, or playing with the cats with a wadded-up ball of paper attached to a string, or working, or sleeping).

What are some last lines you'd bet have *never* been uttered on a deathbed? Here are my suggestions:

1. "I'm really, really sorry I had all that passionate sex when I was young and beautiful."
2. "Why didn't I ever learn how to hem my garments properly?"
3. "I wish there had been many more opportunities to watch *The Weakest Link*."
4. "If only I'd carefully read every issue of *Shape* magazine. . . ."
5. "Why, oh why, didn't I organize my closet according to color and texture of garment?"
6. "That Kia was the best investment I ever made."
7. "I wish I'd learned all the words to the theme songs from *Davy Crockett, Growing Pains,* and *Friends.*"
8. "Why didn't I spend more time playing the nickel slots?"

9. "If only I'd had my hair frosted!"

10. "I wish I had rolled up every single one of my coins into those convenient little paper cylinders. . . ."

11. "Is the picture on my driver's license a good likeness?"

12. "Can I please have one more spoonful of fat-free yogurt?"

13. "Life would have had more meaning if only I'd never broken anything in the kitchen."

14. "I wish I had spent more time alphabetizing my spices."

15. "If only I had mastered the art of decoupage!"

16. "Why, oh why, wasn't I given more time to watch all the reruns of *Celebrity Rehab?*"

17. "If only my combined SAT score had been twenty points higher, I could rest in peace."

18. "Well, I certainly am glad I never told any members of my family that I love them."

19. "Would that there were one last chance for me to understand fully the intricate workings of my George Foreman's Lean Mean Grilling Machine!"

20. "Do you think this shroud will make me look fat?"

22

IS WEDNESDAY NOW SUNDAY?

After any holiday weekend don't you find yourself staggering around wondering what happened to your ordinary life?

I am wholly bamboozled during weeks where holidays fall on Tuesday or Wednesday. When are you supposed to relax? Before or after? If you make it a longish weekend, on which end does the weekend happen?

Let's say you went to work on a day during the summer when everybody else takes the day off; you force your assistant to do the same. The building that you work in is like going to work on Neptune: you and your assistant are the only life-forms around, and even this is stretching it a bit. You are barely life-forms, what with the office not being air-conditioned and your fear of plugging yet one more appliance (an actual working fan) into an already-overloaded single electrical outlet in the wall. In similar circumstances, I have thought of Scotty from *Star Trek*, when the engines were overloaded (which happened about every seventeen minutes), warning Kirk, "We can't push her any further, Captain, or else she'll blow us all to kingdom come!"

It's sort of like that in my office; we're prepared for a meltdown at any moment. My assistant and I, during one of these summer days, have looked like extras from a scene out of one of those old movies where peasant women toil in the fields with bandanas wrapped around their foreheads or wound around their necks. Poor Sarah was working away at the computer, which was cranky because of the heat (the computer, not Sarah), and I was returning phone calls, which was a joke because it became *very* obvious *very* soon that only two other people were working throughout the tri-state area and that both of them planned to leave by 3:00 P.M.

Holiday weeks such as these inevitably bring to mind good old Tom Carvel, and not just because hot weather is synonymous with soft-serve dairy products (although, of course, that is also true). Remember when Mr. Carvel, founder and (I suppose) owner of the ice-cream syndicate, did all the announcements on his own commercials? Mr. Carvel had a voice like traffic, yelled every syllable as if he were talking long distance on a cheap phone, and he had an accent that made Robert De Niro sound like Prince Charles. In these radio advertisements Tom Carvel kept hollering, "*Wednesday is sundae at Carvel's*," but since he was on the radio you couldn't see the spelling of "sundae" and so it sounded like Mr. Carvel was either totally nuts or changing the entire calendar just for the heck of it. What the ad was attempting to communicate, however, was simply that you could buy frozen hot-fudge sundaes (already a genuinely problematic idea in itself) at a discount price if you purchased them on a Wednesday. Or something to that effect. But I was struck to the heart by the thought that if you ran a big enough empire, you could just switch one day of the week for another.

And that seems to be happening during these odd holiday weeks.

Okay, it is true that Monday, Thursday, and Friday holidays pose fewer problems. For example, over Thanksgiving week you get Friday off—unless you are working for one of those stores where the Holiday Horrors begin at 8:00 A.M. the Friday after Thanksgiving. (Forget the scary movies *Halloween* and *Friday the 13th*: anyone who has worked retail knows that "Friday After Thanksgiving" is the most terrifying time of the year. The mention of it alone is enough to solicit muffled yells and barely suppressed screams from those working behind perfume counters and in the lingerie department.)

Tom Carvel, where are you when we need you? Please help me remember that Wednesday is always Wednesday, sundaes and holidays notwithstanding.

23

WHERE'S CARRIE FISHER

WHEN YOU NEED HER?

The one female character with a speaking part in the last *Star Wars* film does exactly two important things: she gets pregnant and dies. That's it.

I never thought I'd say this, but I really miss Carrie Fisher.

Star Wars Episode III: Revenge of the Sith (a title with the unhappy effect of making everyone who discusses the movie sound in desperate need of speech therapy) has the one female character say things such as, "Hold me, Anakin. Hold me like you did on Naboo."

That's how you know the movie is science fiction: on this planet, if you ever say things like that to men, they run away so fast they leave skid marks. What else does she say? She says, in a moment of great turmoil, "You've changed!" This is what she whines when she notices her love interest becoming the Prince of Darkness, the Embodiment of Evil, the Vessel of the Dark Side. I use stronger language when my husband says I should use more garlic in the sauce. If I should ever notice that my husband's eyes were becoming radioactive, as do the eyes of the spoiled, grumpy boy-hero Anakin, I might speak a little more firmly.

Certainly Carrie Fisher's Princess Leia would have used a less pleading, less wimpy tone. As I remember, Leia not only kicked butt (sometimes quite literally) but also had some terrific lines. She was an active, crucial, irreplaceable part of the trio, right alongside Han Solo and Luke Skywalker. She was, in fact, the smart one in that group. Leia didn't whine and snivel like Luke, and she was smart enough to choose Han Solo instead of her brother.

Apart from having bagels over her ears, Leia seems to exercise good judgment. For example, when Han Solo pats himself on the back by announcing, "Not a bad bit of rescuing, huh? You know, sometimes I amaze even myself," Princess Leia instantly replies, "That doesn't sound too hard." Embodying the wit of Dorothy Parker and the timing of Mae West, the original *Star Wars* babe had a feisty, sexy, competitive, complex personality that made a whole generation of little girls want to be her when they ran the galaxy. Who wouldn't want to be the one with the punch line in the following exchange?:

HAN SOLO: Look, Your Worshipfulness, let's get one thing straight.
I take orders from just one person: me.
PRINCESS LEIA: It's a wonder you're still alive.

When little girls want to be the new heroine, Padmé (even the name sounds like a new line of ladies' bras), what is it precisely they'll be doing?

As far as I can tell, she gets knocked up, pops out twins like English muffins from a toaster, and then expires, like a carton of old milk.

The reason Padmé dies, according to the droid doctors who look after her during childbirth, is simply that "she has lost the will to live."

Believe me, if women dropped dead every time they lost the will to live, they'd be sweeping out the bodies from the T.J. Maxx dressing room on an hourly basis during bathing-suit season. (To clarify: Women do not die because we lose the will to live. We drop because we get inadequate health care, with inadequate funding, and because a lot of us have to choose droid doctors approved by our HMO health-care plans. Do I sound bitter? Oh, just hold me like you did on Naboo. . . .)

Padmé is neurasthenic, weird, passive—an annoying character. Not a lot of action for an action figure—and yet there is indeed a Padmé action figure available: a lady with skinny legs, a gun, and an untucked blouse obviously symbolizing advanced pregnancy (the gestation period on this planet being about three weeks—Padmé cooks up those twins quickly and without the addition of any unsightly pounds). Skinny, armed, and pregnant: this is the effect of forty years of the women's movement on American cinema.

And this isn't getting at the larger issue: that the simple presence of the feminine in Anakin Skywalker's life is the catalyst for his turn to the Dark Side. It is because our hero falls in love with Padmé that Anakin goes all weak and evil. So I guess the Catholic Church, John Milton's *Paradise Lost,* and Rush Limbaugh are all proved correct—it is women who plant the seed of disharmony and cause the wreckage of masculine community. Terrific.

And just in case you think anything has changed in the last, oh, twenty years or so, may I remind you what happens to Maggie Gyllenhaal's character in 2008's blockbuster *The Dark Knight*? Rachel Dawes, the woman beloved by Batman, dies. That's right, she gets blown up. The guy in the cape can save the rest of Gotham, but the one broad he loves gets scattered around the city like ticker tape after a parade. What are Rachel's most feisty, strongest, character-driven lines? Like Padmé, this twenty-first century heroine doesn't actually have any.

(True, Rachel does make the following statement in a note to Bruce Wayne—"I will be there, but only as your 'friend.' I'm sorry to let you down. If you lose your faith in me, please keep your faith in people"—and pretty much directly after that gets detonated, which proves that the whole "just friends" line never works the way you think it will.)

I suspect that Carrie Fisher's Princess Leia will continue to carry the crown for defiant, smart, witty heroines for quite some time, and that's fine. But you know what I'd love to see, just for kicks, just to play out this wildly imaginative fantasy I've been carrying around since 1977? I'd love to see a heroine live through the whole movie—not go off a cliff, get buried alive, shot in an alley, covered with crude oil, or defenestrated. Imagine becoming bored with dead heroines the way we've become bored by cute space aliens and sensitive bearded guys! Now *that* would be something to draw women to the theaters; the presentation of triumphant, articulate, and live heroines would be a radical cinematic gesture worth our applause.

24

WHEREVER DID YOU FIND

THAT OUTFIT?

It is a truth universally acknowledged that an intellectual, even one given a clothing allowance, will dress like a schlemiel.

Historically, intellectuals have been the subject of both high and low humor. From the sixth century onward, how we dress has prompted nearly automatic laughter from onlookers, even if the onlookers wore twigs and painted their faces blue. Why are we, as a group, so sartorially impoverished that we make other professionals, even those in actuarial science or previously owned vehicle sales, look good?

(Just to make sure we're all clear about this one point: I include myself in this group. And I am including you, dear reader. Trust me on this one—the following observations are not about other people.)

Look at us. Glance around a room at a professional meeting: we look like refugees. And not refugees from an interesting culture. Refugees from Filenes's Basement in 1999 or from Nordstrom's Rack in 2004. Many intellectuals, who possess the bewildering self-satisfaction of the entirely self-absorbed, will not accept the idea that garments they purchased new in 2001 are now not only unfashionable but also unsavory. In part, our collective reluctance to update our wardrobe proceeds from faulty logic. Whether applied to clothing or to original research and writing, the intellectual often thinks, *Hey, if it was good enough to get me this job, there is no reason to mess with the ideal. I found what fits me. Don't force me to mess with my signature style.*

Do we—those working in publishing, on newspapers, in bookstores, for online publications, in the smarter offices of magazines and production studios, in academic venues and libraries—forfeit any sense of judgment concerning apparel because we spend much of our time with creatures significantly younger than ourselves? After all, the young we hire and mentor are not about to tell us if we are dressing like morons.

Face it: young people don't notice how we look. If we showed up with a hairnet and goggles, the under-thirties wouldn't flinch. Or even react. They pay attention to us because we are at the head of the table, not because we make a snazzy impression. They look at us because they have to. Mostly they see taupe or gray or purple shapes. The only gender distinction is this: straight males can wear the same sports jacket or sweater every Tuesday for thirteen weeks and it will pass without comment, whereas if a female (of any sexual orientation) wears the same suit two times in a row she will be considered slatternly.

Not that the young parade around in gowns and tuxxes; they will show up in pajamas and feel this is peachy. They spend more time worrying about their bodies than what they put on their bodies. Youth these days believe health and beauty to be synonymous.

These sublimely fit gazelles can wear cargo pants and look acutely gorgeous.

Whereas, if we wear cargo pants, we look like cargo.

God knows we cannot expect any help from our bosses in getting ourselves spiffed up. No one sane would ever seek his or her supervisor's advice. You see what those people look like? The dapper ones look like extras from the bar scene in *American Gangster*. The other ones look like extras from the peasant scenes in *Mamma Mia!* Executive intellectuals make ordinary intellectuals look dashing. This, in part, explains why random life-forms who are awarded their own administrative assistants are located as far away as possible from the actual working staff. This is arranged carefully to ensure that the system can continue to operate. If young people newly hired caught even a glimpse of the powers that be, they'd rise up with pitchforks and torches. Best to keep the bosses in their cozy offices and out of view.

Intellectual women look like circus ponies, wearing feathers, tassels, and suits designed by the folks who make clothes for drum majorettes. If a senior intellectual woman should wear a skirt made entirely out of men's shirt collars, for example, she is considered a radical fashionista as well as a feminist goddess. A normal adult woman wearing such an outfit would be regarded as just one frame short of a Looney Tune.

Our men look like inmates only recently released from federal penitentiaries, forced to wear clothing at least fifteen years out of style. They wear oddly colored cashmere sweaters. These items, never flattering, now fit them around the middle like tea cozies. They have been known to wear clogs. They sometimes wear, for pity's sake, berets.

Blurring the lines between gender and generation but in no way stepping into the world of good taste, the self-proclaimed hip among us wear dusty and unmatched black, as if being inducted into a religious order or proceeding to a funeral. Or a hanging. Lots of intellectuals look as if we are waiting to be hanged.

Of course, this might only incidentally have to do with clothing.

Not that I'm bitter.

Infant intellectuals eschew the pink and blue blankets in favor of gender-neutral yellows and subversive greens. They are one of the few groups of toe suckers to understand fully the importance of their feminized pre-Oedipal experiences. Their dislike for the more garish interpretations of universal mythologies—a refusal to accept My Little Pony as a representation of equine desirability, or a pronounced lack of enthusiasm for the spiritually gorier episodes of *SpongeBob SquarePants*—is indicative of an uncompromising commitment to the definitive restructuring of the whole infantalization of babies, so pervasive in contemporary American culture. It is time to stand up to such outmoded belief systems, the baby intellectual seems to be articulating, except of course that "standing up" and "speaking" are no more possible for the infant than, say, "continence"—which itself could be regarded as a locus not of liberation but of domination by the sophisticated, culturally aware wee scholar.

Infant intellectuals grow into kids who hover, socially, on the barely acceptable fringe of school life. Yes, photographs of adolescent intellectuals appear in our senior yearbooks. But unless we edited these volumes, we do not figure prominently. We rarely cheerled; we rarely slam-dunked; we rarely kicked ass in any visible way. Instead, we ran the student papers and debate teams; we got supporting roles in theatrical productions of *Bye-Bye Birdie;* we formed the school's first creative writing clubs. We were the ones using mimeograph machines after class or Xeroxing clandestinely in the Main Office. We cut our own hair. We wore Keds and wrote in ink all over them. We graffitied ourselves but rarely gratified ourselves.

We kept journals. We kept journals remorselessly. We turned "journaling" into a verb, for which we should be shot.

Later we pioneered open-mike nights and poetry slams. We wore heavy black eye makeup and we never ironed.

We batiked. We taught ourselves guitar. We sang "Blackbird Singing in the Dead of Night" from the White Album and went on to warble and destroy songs by Eric Clapton, the Roches, and Shawn Colvin. We wanted Spanish boots of Spanish leather (or Pleather, if we were strict), and motorcycle jackets (motorcycle not included), and old silk shawls. Later we wanted Tintin wristwatches from Parisian street vendors, black feather boas from the East Village, and Doc Martens from old friends in Clapham

Junction. Throughout all, we exhibited a lingering fondness for scarves, retro eyeglasses, and hats. (Our closets simply crawl with chapeaux.)

Such costuming in boots and boas is an offshoot of the way we pined for adventure; we longed to be outlaws. We read promiscuously and imagined ourselves the hero or heroine (or both) in every text and had been doing so since our first *Pat the Bunny*. Our big mistake, however, was thinking we could look like these heroes and heroines.

We were gloomy, saturnine young men patterned after Hawthorne, Hemingway, Ted Hughes, Tom Wolfe, or Sam Shepard yet oddly indistinguishable from one another when brushing up against cash bars at professional meetings. Even when dressed in summer colors, we resembled crows circling carrion. Our shoes were rarely polished; our socks almost always slipped. When we danced, which was more often than we liked to admit, we looked less like Mick Jagger or David Bowie than John Cleese doing a funny walk.

We were women dressing as closely as humanly possible to Jane Austen, Virginia Woolf, Sylvia Plath, or Susan Sontag, all moving toward the shrimp appetizer platters the way hyenas move in for a kill. We wore clunky jewelry that looked like small ceramic ashtrays strung together by a class of slow children. We thought our hair was tousled; it was actually ratty. When we danced, which was as often as possible, we looked less like Joan Jett or Stevie Nicks than a circle of jiggling postmenopausal naiads.

In seeking to dress to please ourselves, we sometimes disguise ourselves. We go out of our way to make ourselves as unlike the fuddy-duddy mentors we once had and, by so doing, make ourselves into the fuddy-duddy mentors of today.

Why is how we dress important, after all? Don't we pride ourselves in saying, along with Hamlet, "I know not seams," winking at the homonym, as if to say we know better than to mistake fripperies for fundamentals? We shouldn't. Because every time we select a shirt, choose a jacket, pick an overcoat, or grab one of the many hats we wear, we make a statement about ourselves.

I'm hoping that the statement I make is not "I dress this way because I am an intellectual and don't know any better. Please be kind."

25

WHY CHILDLESS WOMEN

MAKE GOOD MOTHERS

$British$ $writer$ $Nancy$ $Mitford$ came up with one of my favorite quotations about women's deep relationships to motherhood: "I love children, especially when they cry, for then someone takes them away."

Some women are born mothers, some achieve motherhood, and some have motherhood thrust upon them.

In strictly historical terms, most women probably had motherhood thrust upon them, what with a lack of reliable birth control for the first couple of thousand years of our species. Only recently has motherhood been one of many options for females who want to fool around. In the past, it was pretty much how my grandmother (mother of nine) described it: "If you wanna have sex, then you're gonna stay home for the next twenty years." I thought she meant "stay home" as in "luxuriate in a totally fulfill-ing domestic environment" when what she meant was "not leave the house without a small child attached to your person until you hit menopause." Only in her later years did she sum up her own childbearing philosophy: "Everybody thought I was sexy. But, to be honest, I was only very bad at math."

But just as fish are not necessarily the best authorities on water, so mothers are not necessarily the best authorities on the causes and effects of motherhood.

"Caus*es*?" you might be saying, with an emphasis on the plural. "Did they invent another way to get pregnant while I was out of town?"

But indeed there are lots of ways to become a mother. There are also lots of ways to locate and adopt a mother for your own personal use when the original one is, for whatever distressing reason, no longer on your schedule.

I've always considered myself a mother, absence of young chil-dren notwithstanding. I look like somebody's mother, I sound like anybody's mother, and heaven knows I act like *everybody's* mother. I advise, I worry, I scold, I applaud, and then I worry some more. As a professor, I consider myself the mother of about a hundred and fifty kids every year—and all of them are in college. I just thank God I am not responsible for their tuition. Or their janito-rial services.

My students line up outside my office door at all hours, as if I were some kind of emotional ATM. True, I am consulted primarily about English department and university issues, but I also hear sto-ries about family difficulties, relationship problems, and financial predicaments. I am asked to give fashion advice ("don't pierce what can't easily be unpierced" is my latest mantra). Decorating advice ("never buy a used futon"). Advice on how a young woman can get the best deal at a used-car lot ("bring a guy, or at least be accompanied by a girl with a very short haircut"); also how a genuinely nice young man with no obvious scarring can convince a young woman of his acquaintance to give him the time of day ("forgetaboutit").

My opinions on matters of the heart, soul, and pocketbook are sought by those not yet calloused enough to understand that, in all three areas, only the head and gut reactions of those involved actually matter. This sort of incidental mothering is one of the best things I do.

I have a suspicion that "incidental mothering" is as close to raising a child as many women should get. Not that I haven't experienced what my friend Karen calls baby lust. But just as almost everybody loves kittens (even those who don't particularly like cats), everybody loves babies, even those who would not be especially good at the daunting and demanding job of actually raising babies to adulthood.

As an unbiased observer of children past the babyGap stage, I can say without the risk of traumatizing any one individual: kids, especially after they exhibit signs of their actual personalities, are exhausting. I suspect that mothers everywhere deserve far more applause than anyone in an MBA program has *ever* received for the accomplishment of helping the youth of America manage their own business.

Because I do not have small children to raise, I can also be as neurotic as I wish without fearing that a minor under my aegis will carry lifelong scars. This is important since children envision even the most normal of women as desperate creatures, which means that I would have been regarded with more than mild trepidation as a primary caregiver. You think I'm exaggerating? Have you ever met an interesting person who declared, without hesitation, "My mom? She was the happiest woman you could ever meet."

No, all intelligent children believe their mothers to be, at best, unfulfilled and, at worst, worthy of portrayal by the erstwhile Tony Perkins or the *The Real Housewives of Orange County*. Nobody *cool* ever had a happy mother. Yet few mothers have ever described themselves, at least in public, as "wildly unhappy" about the assigned role as "mom." Line up the numbers and the meaning is clear: somebody is lying. (I'm not passing judgment here; I'm only reporting the facts.) The point is that certain folks were chosen by destiny to be biological parents while other folks were chosen to listen to those parents when they needed to whine.

If childless women make good mothers to the young, we also make dandy mothers to mothers. We do not judge or evaluate their parenting skills against our own. If a friend calls me up and says, "The baby has been crying since March and I am now going to put her in the linen closet so that I can take a shower," she knows I'm not thinking, *What a terrible mother. I never even thought of putting little Emma in the pantry until she cried for an entire season.* My friend is confident that I'm thinking, in contrast, *Ohgodohgod, please let everybody be okay. And thank you for allowing other women to accept the burden of motherhood while I just get to teach kids about literature and the inherent dangers of piercing and the serious mistake of even considering the purchase of a used futon.*

26

WHY IS NOSTALGIA NOT LIKE IT
USED TO BE?

It might just be my girlish way of looking at things, but I loathe magazines that depict an Olde Worlde where big cheery families were always happily sitting inside vaguely rough-hewn but immaculately clean wooden buildings, sitting at richly adorned tables, chatting companionably while a cheery fire lit their healthy, rosy cheeks with a warm glow—up until contemporary life ruined everything.

These magazines make it sound as if all of family life was one big Hallmark card scenario until modern life stepped in. . . . Stepped in with what, exactly?

With its silly modern antibiotics and pesky vitamins? With its overly clean water and ridiculous reliance on lead-free utensils?

With its rotten habit of properly cooking foods and ridding most meals of salmonella?

Am I the only one to think that maybe such celebrations of the good old days are a tad misleading?

Such articles make it seem as if stringing cranberries is an activity so spiritually and emotionally meaningful that in and of itself it would compensate for, let's say, the lack of running water in a household. As if eating by candlelight would be so romantic that nobody would mind the fact that it was forty-six degrees inside the house.

As if wearing homespun clothing would outweigh the lack of antiperspirant, deodorant, not to mention a whole other concept of what we would call in our horrible modern manner basic hygiene. This was a world without toilet paper or, for that matter, toilets. You had to pee in a pot under your bed at night and then bring it outside the next day. For some of us who don't like to use a restroom when there's anybody within six feet of us to act as a witness, what do you think it would have been like to drag your chamber pot down through the kitchen in the morning? This was a world without tampons, people. This was not a fun place to be a girl.

Nostalgia, when rabid (and there was rabies, too; don't forget rabies), would encourage us to believe that having a taffy pull for the whole family would keep us from realizing that very few of the family actually had their own teeth. ("Give that last piece of pork to little Martha. Her canines are still workin' good. She can gnaw on that for the rest of the evenin' and it'll keep her quiet.")

This is probably also the place to mention that having a big family was not exactly something you could prevent from happening. I mean, once you started having a family, you kept having family. There was no central heating. There were no indoor lights. No cable. And a person can only pull so much taffy.

Therefore, I am compelled to offer thanks for what we all too often take for granted in our gloriously modern age, including but not limited to the following:

- Zippers
- Mattresses, ones not made from straw ("don't let the bedbugs bite!" was once not a cutesy saying—it was a profound wish)
- Aspirin
- Ice cubes
- Electric lights, but not those horrible curly ones; I hate those and refuse to believe they will save the planet
- Toothpaste, toothbrushes, and people who use them
- Hairbrushes not made from the bristles of large porcine creatures
- Ballpoint pens
- Soap not made from the fat of large porcine creatures
- Clocks you do not have to remember to wind (okay, maybe one is nice, but the others should actually function like clockwork)
- Disposable tissues, so that handkerchiefs can be kept for both their correct uses: blotting one's tears prettily while watching *Wuthering Heights* (the one with Laurence Olivier) or attending

the wedding of a male friend you might have married had life
turned out just that little bit differently

- Pots and pans with handles that do not instantly heat up and take
off three layers of skin when you forget to use a massive oven
mitt made from the bristles of large porcine creatures

- Oven mitts

- Ovens that don't need to be stoked (actually, a life free from devices that need stoking is a leap forward)

- The absolutely adorable fact that certain groups of human beings
are not legally enslaved to others

- The *other* absolutely adorable fact that certain groups of human
beings are not legally burnt as witches, driven from their com-
munities as deviants, or tarred and feathered as embodiments of
seditious wickedness

- Mascara that you don't have to brush out of that red flat May-
belline container your mother had to use when you were little,
even though it was kind of cool to watch her use the little black
brush on her eyelashes, especially if she let you play with the
tiny brush afterward and maybe even use it for your dolls if you
were good and promised not to play with it when she wasn't
looking (the brushes were probably made from the bristles of
rather small porcine creatures)

- Immodium

- Staples

- Adhesive tape

- Votes for women

- Erasers

- Telephone answering machines that allow you hear who is calling before you have to pick up so that you don't have to speak to your sister about her new weight-loss program unless you really want to discuss it
- A new generation of SSRIs, which might, if only she would listen to you, help your sister stop obsessing about her weight
- Closets
- Vacuum cleaners
- Pencil sharpeners
- The eradication of several childhood diseases, so that even if your kids don't adorably trill, "Look, dearest Mamma, at how sweetly Sister and I string popcorn, not to mention cranberries, as we sing carols by the fire," they also don't say, "Too bad we both have rickets, caused by a profound lack of vitamin D"
- Indoor showers, or outdoor showers, for that matter
- Fluffy towels not made from the bristles of large porcine creatures
- Shoes that decorate and comfort the feet; footwear that does more than cover your appendages in order to protect them from the layers of mud, ice, and rock lurking directly outside your door in the unpaved street, not to mention helping to put a barrier between your feet and the human and animal waste you'll find there; footwear with, for example, a sexy strap across the ankle.

27

HOW TO READ YOUR REUNION

YEARBOOK

When you announce that there's a reunion coming up, people will start offering you advice. They'll tell you to lose weight, find a new partner, get your hair dyed/done, get new contacts (for your eyes and also for your professional life), but I have a different set of suggestions. Mine involve *not* the attending of the event itself—really, don't you have better things to do, and, really, do you want to bother with the diet right now?—but also the equally harrowing experience you'll face when you get the updated "Reunion Yearbook." The *book* you can't ignore.

The following pointers will help you navigate, negotiate, and maneuver through this most complicated of life's passages.

1. Look up serious old boyfriends. Discover that two of them have married beautiful women at least twenty years their— and your—junior. Realize this means that they have married girls who could have been your daughter had you and the boyfriend stayed together and gotten married right after college, which you might have done if things had gone just a tiny bit differently that spring weekend. Wonder if there are state laws against such things as incest-by-proxy. Become unnerved when doing the math and discovering twenty years younger than you is not so young anymore. Learn that the one other serious old boyfriend is now a fitness guru describing himself as "deeply into recovery" after a series of relationships with "objectionable, demanding, unhealthy women." Decide that for a fitness guru he doesn't look so hot. Doesn't he look a lot like Ed Koch, only even less stylish? Puzzle about how you could have missed it.

2. Look up less important old boyfriends. Note that two have changed sexual preference. See that another is "in development" on a new cable station devoted to the "needs of females"; he is proud to announce he will be sole executive producer once Fallopian Tube: Television for Babes with a Grudge is on the air. Three remaining old boyfriends have disappeared, apparently without providing any forwarding information to the class secretary or, if your memory of them is any indication of their current status in life, their parole officers.

3. Look up your erstwhile rivals. Establish immediately that all of them are thinner, happier, and more successful than you. Your worst enemy either still looks like a lap dancer or is mar-

ried to a woman who looks like one. See your rivals surrounded by beautiful children (ones they've had, not ones they've married), clones of themselves at eighteen, during their latest alpine skiing trip—the one organized as a surprise by their devoted spouse in celebration of their twenty-second wedding anniversary. See them winning the National Book Award. See them opening a wild-animal refuge on their family estate, thereby "giving back to the land" what their predecessors robbed from it. See them owning most of Maui. Feel same old lurid sense of combined envy and resentment rise in throat. Some things, unlike glaciers or the positions of stars, do not change over time.

4. Look up people you feel guilty about: the girls who wanted to be better friends with you than you wanted to be with them because you feared their nerdiness, sadness, or slowness would cramp your style, which was sort of a moot point because "style" was not really anything you contained in huge quantities; the sweet, funny, but unattractive guys who hung around but never made it to the dating rung even though at that point in your life you would have been far wiser to have been involved with them than the morons who somehow managed to capture your attention (see items 1 and 2 above); the roommate who got moved out of the triple when you and the other, sharper roommate decided to relocate; the kid who let you copy all the notes in Geology I ("Rocks for Jocks") and you promised to take out to dinner but never did; the kid who smelled funny. Observe that each and every one of these is also happier and more successful than you. Also thinner. (NB:

All the guys you didn't date are not only handsome but also in excellent physical condition. They look lots better than Soupy The Guru, for example.) Come to terms with the fact that the kid who smelled funny is now the CEO of a software company with a larger annual budget than that of the Dominican Republic. Realize your lack of intimacy in no way seemed to unduly bother any of these folks. Surprise yourself by feeling relieved rather than resentful.

5. Look up the dead. Be humbled as well as daunted by the number. Get out your freshman yearbook and look them up. Have your breath taken away as you see their smiling teenage faces. Realize you knew many of them, if not by name then by sight. At least five were in classes with you. Another three were in your dorm complex. You probably said "hi" and maybe laughed together when the professor made a lame joke. They are ahead of you now, having skipped the last few years. Find yourself hoping they'll remember you when you arrive on *their* campus.

28

WHERE HAVE ALL THE

BRECK GIRLS GONE?

Canisters featured largely in the fancier kitchens I visited in my youth. It seemed a decidedly American thing, this business of pouring stuff from a bag laboriously into a smaller container that had a rooster painted on the side. None of my aunts had such elegant articles in their kitchens, so I assumed matching canisters were out of our league, along with rumpus rooms, shag rugs, and elaborately representational Jell-O molds. We didn't have those niceties, either.

Everybody else seemed to have them, however. I swore as a kid that every home in America had the following items, necessities my family insanely chose to live without: telephone tables, Bonomo Turkish Taffy, chafing dishes, a used IBM typewriter, carbon paper, knit toilet-paper holders, Maypo, and Prell.

I especially fetishized the idea of both TV dinners and Shake'n Bake. Neither of these was ever available to me. My Italian family would no more have served a TV dinner—even to a child—than they would have served human remains. The very thought of putting chicken pieces into a Baggie of pre-measured spices would have caused my grandmother to clutch her heart and lean against the kitchen table until somebody brought her espresso to calm her down. Yes, that's what we used espresso for in my house, so you can just imagine how serene it always was when I was growing up.

Recently I heard that whoever was responsible for Prell shampoo was no longer going to be manufacturing the space-age substance. If you're too young to remember the seminal advertisement, it offered scientific proof that Prell could do practically everything but prevent heart attacks, it was so amazing. As I recall, the ad showed a green viscous liquid (a detail that you would notice only if you were over a friend's house and that friend's family possessed the new miracle of Color Television). This quasi-liquid Prell substance was so remarkable that it would cause a pearl to float slowly to the bottom of the container. (NB: I still have no idea what that proved about what on earth would happen to your hair, but it was mesmerizing and I recall the image vividly.)

Forget the snows of yesteryear: where have the Breck Girls and Toni Twins gone? Do only their hairdressers know for sure?

This started me thinking about all that *stuff* that once seemed essential to life and no longer captures the public imagination—stuff that is only found in the dusty back aisles of megastores if indeed it (or they) can be found at all. How could *stuff* we once couldn't live without now be scarce? Or worse, simply unimportant?

Didn't everybody once rely on the following (listed in no particular hierarchy) for health and happiness: mothballs, camphor, iodine, mercurochrome, metal ice trays, Bosco, smelling salts, record players (and those little plastic inserts you had to use to play a 45 on a regular, grown-up record player), Brylcreem, three-martini lunches, wooden clothespins, cap guns, carpet sweepers, the Fuller Brush Man, the Avon lady (coming door-to-door and ringing the bell and giving real little lipstick samples), reel-to-reel tape recorders, Tang, pipe cleaners, a really good butcher, Accent food enhancer, vinyl doorknob covers, mercury thermometers (fragile things of beauty that would break into wonderful—albeit deadly—tiny drops of elusive, living silver), double features, rabbit ear TV antennas, test patterns, dialing telephones (meaning: there was an actual "dial"; this gave meaning to the term "dial tone," which is now a hugely ridiculous misnomer), sheer hairnets that ladies actually slept in, big plastic curlers, Baked Alaska, fallout shelters, bridge tables, flash cubes, wax paper, clothes brushes, and Bromo-Seltzer?

Didn't you once think you needed Tame, Psssssst, a girdle, a half slip, and a bra that lifted and separated in order to look merely presentable? (I direct this specifically to women readers, but what the heck, anybody can answer.) Didn't you think grown-up ladies went to Jack LaLanne, drank Metrecal, and used panty hose with "tummy control" panels? Didn't you think you needed "Modess . . . because." (Personally I spent the five years between learning to read and seeing that movie shown to girls in the fifth grade trying to figure out "because *why*???")

Didn't men wear hats—one for winter and one for summer—and real hats, not baseball caps? Didn't men wear short-sleeved T-shirts under their regular shirts, like the genuine pieces of underwear they were meant to be? Didn't men smoke pipes? Shine their shoes with Kiwi shoe polish? Use those palm-held flat brushes to groom their hair? When was the last time you heard an adult man even use the word "groom" when he wasn't talking about a wedding? Was that man smoking a pipe? Wearing a half slip?

Was he talking to the Toni Twins? Did any of them—or any of us—realize that the word "permanent" is not linked to actual "permanence"?

Sing it with me: where have all the Breck Girls gone?

29

IS FEMINISM'S THEME SONG STILL

"YES, WE HAVE NO BANANAS"?

Let's say you're heading up to a light. When it begins to change to yellow, although you notice it, naturally enough, you still expect the car ahead of you to proceed. You put your foot on the gas because instinct and experience dictate that you're staying in motion. But the person ahead of you suddenly stops. Maybe the car stalled or slipped between gears, or maybe the driver perceived a danger outside your line of vision. You slam into the car.

Instead of being in an organized progression what you find yourself in is a bit of a wreck.

And not because you're some demolition-derby fanatic intent on destroying whatever is in your way, either. Nothing that dramatic. Of course you should have been paying more attention. Suddenly, however, the whomping punch of an immovable object being hit by the unstoppable Subaru brings you to your senses. Only upon impact do you recognize you're now part of a chain reaction (the driver behind you now having enthusiastically tapped your bumper). And without anybody having meant any harm, there's now a pileup.

Contemporary feminist thought is now in that pileup. It's not so much that we're in a backlash as we're in a whiplash.

We expected smoother passage into the future once we got the green light (the vote, control over our reproductive functions, access to education and employment goals historically regarded as unreachable for those with breasts). We got rooms of our own, credit lines of our own, and the right to our own pinup calendars of hunky firefighters—and we insist on saying "fire fighters" and not "firemen" because even as we stare at shoulders and abs we don't want to perpetuate a sexist trope.

Yet instead of moving forward with confidence we find ourselves in a wreck. Nothing fatal, thank god, but enough to slow us down and to cause a certain self-satisfied rubbernecking on the part of those not directly involved.

Let me explain.

We would have thought after forty years of feminist theory, the publications not only of *The Second Sex* and *The Feminine Mystique* but also of *Sexual Politics*, *Fear of Flying*, *The Madwoman in the Attic*, and two (count 'em) editions of *The Norton Anthology of Women's Literature,* things would be different. Remember that we grew up when the song "I Will Follow Him" was already an oldie ("following the guy wherever he may go" made it sound as if he should enter a Witness Protection Program to get away from somebody he dated once). Instead we grew up having danced the night away to Gloria Gaynor's belting out "I Will Survive," to Annie Lennox's pointing out that "sisters are doin' it for themselves," and to Tina Turner's asking directly, "What's love got to do with it?" So if we weren't exactly racing ahead, at the very least we were moving along (with some rhythm, yet) at a steady clip.

We got to college, where we picked up books and dropped our drawers. We read Claude Lévi-Strauss and Sherry B. Ortner; we read the *Story of O* and *The Sensuous Woman,* by "J." By the 1970s, virginity seemed as outdated as a rubber girdle. Chastity, as defined by anthropologists and sociologists, was regarded as the cornerstone where capitalism met patriarchy.

Instead of revering the hymen as a manifest symbol of spiritual worth, we thought of it as something like baby fat, part of yourself you'd lose once you started to grow up. The very idea of it seemed quaint. We wore T-shirts that announced: "I lost my virginity, but I still have the box it came in."

Maybe it was just our girlish way of looking at things, but we thought life would be better for women—and men, yes, we thought it would improve for men, too—when women were seen as being productive rather than merely reproductive members of society. We imagined that the saw edge of patriarchy would be worn down, its teeth filed flat; we thought that so-called traditional values would go the way of the AMC Gremlin, given that they proved to be destructive, poorly designed, and incredibly uncomfortable for the long haul.

We could not have anticipated that in a few decades there would emerge medical practices in major metropolitan centers specializing in "hymenoplasty," the reconstruction of that small membrane. For a fairly hefty fee, a woman can, for example, now choose to "repair and tighten the hymen to a more virgin-like state."

When consulting Web sites about this procedure, I was struck with the repeated asking of a sample question: "How far in advance should I schedule my hymen repair?" to which of course the only reasonable answer is "Before somebody pops your cherry; otherwise it counts as elective surgery and you're going to need to pay with your Discover card."

Even when the medical information provided explains that virginity itself cannot be restored—since virginity for both men and women is defined as the state existing only before actual sexual intercourse—these Web sites nevertheless emphasize that not only is their surgery virtually undetectable but also that indeed their mission is to "empower women with knowledge, choice, and alternatives."

Apart from women living within cultures where they can be tortured or killed for not bleeding on their wedding night— women who, I suspect, might not have the necessary $5K in cash to pony up for the procedure—doesn't this seem like less than an "empowering alternative"?

If getting your hymen altered is sort of like taking your vagina in for a tune-up because you're trying to fix the numbers on the odometer and you have the temerity to see this as "empowerment," then you are most accurately described by an article that appeared in *The Onion* in 2003, titled "Women Now Empowered by Everything a Woman Does." *The Onion* satirizes the trend to re-gard everything the typical woman does as an act of "empower-ment":

> [According to Barbara Klein,] "As recently as 15 years ago, a woman could only feel empowered by advancing in a male-dominated work world, asserting her own sexual wants and needs, or pushing for a stronger voice in politics. Today, a woman can empower herself through actions as seemingly inconsequential as driving her children to soccer practice or watching the Oxygen network."
>
> [*The Onion* goes on to claim:] Whereas early feminists campaigned tirelessly for improved health care and safe, legal access to abortion, often against a backdrop of public indif-ference or hostility, today's feminist asserts control over her biological destiny by wearing a baby-doll T-shirt with the word "Hoochie" spelled in glitter."

Little did we think, when Madonna first wore torn-up lace fishnet tights and sang "Like a Virgin," that in twenty years mega-stores would be selling lines of clothes to actual little girls making them look like actual little hookers. Sure, it's almost inevitable that what once passed for invention and freedom gets co-opted and exploited by the established economic and power structure, but somehow we didn't think it was going to happen to us. We didn't think that telling girls they shouldn't feel any shame about their bodies or sexual urges would mean that our daughters (or our granddaughters or kid sisters) would be eagerly participating in blow-job parties at age twelve.

What the hell have we been doing?

Have we just been revving our engines all this time or, as Eric Clapton might say, sitting in idle much too long? Why else, after all these years, are we still making ourselves crazy over the following topics?:

1. Why there is a gender-specific discrepancy in how we clean countertops
2. Why most women feel guilty about everything and men about nothing
3. Why the complexity of the female orgasm is comparable to the complexity of, say, Chartres Cathedral
4. Whether the embrace of motherhood and the achievement of professional success are mutually exclusive
5. Is it biology that makes women flush public toilets with our feet or else wrap the handle with so much toilet paper—in order to prevent contact with our actual fingers—that whole hectares of rain forest are denuded during every second-act intermission?

Okay, let's look at orgasms, particularly those defined as "fake." It has always been my assumption that, as with pearls and love, there is no such thing as a "fake" version: either they are pearls or they are paste; either it is love or it isn't ("true love" being an unexamined and therefore insidious oxymoron).

In contrast, nowhere in books about men and culture do we see discussed the issue of men's fake orgasms. If you ask even the most self-aware, emotionally evolved, "This is what a feminist looks like" T-shirt-wearing guy whether men should fake orgasms, he will give you a blank stare. "Why would a guy do that?" he stammers. He knows it's a trick question.

When hunting the sometimes elusive female orgasm—which is like hunting for Bigfoot, but different—we often end up hearing that, like parallel parking or establishing lines of credit, orgasms are easier for men than for women. Why is this not a shock? Why don't I think huge sums of valuable grant money should be used to prove this particular point over and over again?

As far as I can tell, women fake orgasms for the same reason men fake sleep: to be left alone. How many women have anxiously asked a man with closed eyes, "Are you awake, sweetie?" only to hear the simulacra of a snore? Faking is a way of saying, "Quit trying to get a response out of me. Enough already."

Our intimate lives still confound the great thinkers, male and female, of our day. And if wondering why we're not coming faster causes us anxiety, we're even more anxious about why we're not getting places more quickly.

Why haven't women, individually and collectively, made it to the checkered flag in every race? Do we spend too much time worrying about others to be successful, or are we most successful when we worry about others? And perhaps most important, if we aren't dazzlingly successful, then whom can we blame?

Ourselves? Too easy. Yeah, sure, but why are we like this?

When asked "What makes women happy?" British novelist Fay Weldon replies, with alacrity, "Nothing, not for more than ten minutes at a time. Anxiety, doubt and guilt break through."

And why, exactly, are we guzzling the guilt the way a Hummer guzzles gas? What does it feed in us? Do we practice recreational self-deprecation and crisis management in order to both hobble ourselves and make the limitations of others seem less distressing? No wonder we seem to be playing bumper cars rather than riding down the highway of life. And when we are riding down the highway of life, we're afraid that we'll end up like Thelma and Louise.

We're so anxious about everything that sometimes we skip the pleasure and go straight to the guilt.

So what do we need to hear? What can help us get all that pleasure that's apparently waiting for us, right outside our self-limiting reach? What women still need to know is that we're not loony, we're not alone, we're not absurd or unprotected, and we need to remind ourselves that we're not going anywhere by standing still.

We need to recalibrate; we need to stop excoriating ourselves for the tiniest of actions and to stop congratulating ourselves for them as well.

For example, we need to get over banana-eating getting-fat guilt—while simultaneously admitting that exercise routines should not be regarded as evidence of moral strength or spiritual virtue, even when they are done on a yoga mat.

We need to stop obsessing over hymens, husbands, and hangnails and once again direct our attention outward to the larger issues of financial equity, economic justice, and the creation of genuinely significant opportunities for women in all workplaces, because some breakthroughs are more important than others.

We need to pass along to the next generation a primer—an owner's manual, if you will—that includes information on how to navigate in all conditions. And it's time for us to get the hell out of this annoying intersection and onto the wide-open highway, after all.

30

ARE YOU A FOOD HYPOCRITE?

"*Fried eggs?!*" Mel's otherwise lovely boyfriend was horrified when she prepared him breakfast. "Are you trying to kill me?"

"B-b-b-ut . . . ," Mel stuttered in response, "I thought that as a special treat, even your high cholesterol could stand a couple of eggs. They're little eggs," she offered.

Even though I'm a firm believer in being grateful toward anyone who will cook you food in the morning, I was on the boyfriend's side in this case.

"The guy has fears about his diet, right?" I shrugged. "You should respect that he's trying to stay healthy."

"What about the four sausages he had the night before?" was Mel's rejoinder.

"Well, he is English," I reminded her, "and they grow up believing that sausage is good for you. I think it's translated into Latin and inscribed over buildings dating back as far as 1430."

"Yeah, well, if you're trying to watch your weight," she pointed out, "fatty meat is not exactly up there with *chai* tea as a good choice."

She had a name for what her lovely young man was engaging in: FOOD HYPOCRISY.

Food hypocrisy is where you tell yourself that you are a moral, virtuous, and pure creature because you don't eat certain food-stuffs.

For example, I'm not a big fan of candy. It is, therefore, re-markably easy for me to feel like I'm the embodiment of healthy living when I eschew Snickers bars. When I buy my husband a Snickers bar, in fact, I feel like I'm supplying him with a danger-ous substance.

In contrast, I could live entirely and solely on cheese and cheese-based products. I wouldn't even need crackers. For me, cheese does indeed stand alone, as per the farmer in the dell. My husband thinks that my obsession with cheese is not only unhealthy but also indeed a sign of a sort of dairy dependency he finds un-nerving.

Food hypocrisy takes a number of forms. Ever go out with somebody who orders a Caesar salad and becomes sanctimonious because something leafy and green is on his or her plate? Such people will not believe that the caloric content of a really good Caesar salad is almost exactly the same as a pepperoni pizza be-cause eating romaine lettuce gives them a *feeling* of virtue. They lose weight with every crunch of crouton—*but only in their brains.*

And hey, if you're a Caesar salad fan, that's terrific, enjoy, may Caesar himself smile upon you, but if you're doing it for a sense of smugness that certain salad eaters radiate, then you're sunk.

How about the Canceling-Out Effect, whereupon a diet soda cancels out the French fries, where stalks of celery cancel out the onion dip, where strawberries cancel out the ice cream?

Yet another subset of food hypocrisy is food substitution, where you eat four bowls of bran cereal and, once you recover, eat two pounds of chocolate to soothe yourself. Food substitution is most often explored in the workplace, where Wheat Thins and V-8 are inhaled in fits of self-discipline, but frozen cheesecakes are devoured in their entirety once the poor soul actually reaches home.

If you eat rice cakes all day—let's face it—you will not be happy, especially if it's not rice cakes that you crave. And who craves rice cakes? You will feel a perfectly human need to compensate for the rice cakes by eating s'mores, telling yourself it is merely another rice product, even if these s'mores have been hidden in the back of the pantry since 1992. (You put them there in order to forget about them so you wouldn't be tempted to eat them. You may have forgotten your first husband's name, but you never forgot where the s'mores were.)

Yogurt is never going to make you feel like you actually ate. Not even frozen yogurt. Not even the kind where there's crunchy stuff on top.

So what's our lesson for today? I'm not suggesting that we use Homer Simpson as a model for healthy eating habits, but I do think we should be grateful for the privilege of being able to eat when we're hungry. And we should be amazed at the luck of being able to choose what we eat. Throughout most of history, only royalty had that privilege. We get to do it every time we go to a Dunkin' Donuts or a smoothie stand. We just shouldn't kid ourselves about what we want and why we want it. Food hypocrisy is dangerous.

Personally, I would never fall into that trap. Unless of course it was baited with cheese.

31

FIFTY-TWO THINGS I LEARNED

BY FIFTY-ONE

1. There is one line that has never been spoken by any man to any woman in the history of civilization. No man has ever said the following: "Let's have a frank and honest discussion about your definition of love because I want to make certain I comprehend fully your every nuanced pause, your every sidelong glance, and your every unuttered sigh." The other line no man has ever said is, "Let's have a candid discussion about wrinkles."

2. Major pharmaceutical companies are missing out by not putting funny sayings on estrogen patches. I'd love a set with "If you can read this, you are too close" or "Ride it like you stole it" printed on them.

3. Just because it fits you doesn't necessarily mean you'll look good in it. If you want proof, look at people anchoring the local news.

4. Just because it is on sale doesn't necessarily mean it's a bargain. Pro-rate what you wear; if you buy a $150 pair of shoes from Taryn Rose and wear them every day, they will end up being cheaper than a pair of $37 shoes from Payless that make the back of your heels bleed so that you have to plaster Band-Aids on yourself like somebody putting posters up on a column or else require you to tape your ankles with "invisible" packing tape as if you were a Thoroughbred expected to win at Belmont in the fifth race, which means that you will wear the shoes once, thus basically blowing $37 to torture yourself. Better to save for a nicer pair. See?

5. You can save yourself an hour a day by not wondering whether you said something stupid in an e-mail, a voice mail, or during a conversation over drinks. Use that time to do something more useful, such as surfing the Net to read about celebrity divorces—after all, any activity is more useful than second-guessing yourself. (Except scrapbooking. Scrapbooking is less useful.) Have you ever compared a woman and a man as they leave a message on a machine canceling a meeting? Man leaves a message: *(Ding)* "It's Bob. That Tuesday at two o'clock, I need to move it. We'll make it Wednesday at four or Thursday at nine. Give me a call. Bye." A woman has to change a meeting: "Hi, it's Marjorie; oh God, I hoped I would get you and not the machine. Okay, I'm sorry, something came up on Tuesday. I know how

busy your schedule is, but something really important, not that our meeting isn't important; our meeting *is* important. But somebody's coming in from out of the country, who was just released from an institution, and I need to meet that person, and I, oh, oh, okay, what?" *(Ding.)* Pause. *(Ding.)* ". . . Hi, it's Marjorie again. Oh, I'm taking up your whole machine. . . ."

6. If you cry when your boyfriend is away on vacation, you might need to reconsider how the term "feminist" applies to you.

7. When you do nice things for people, what will most often happen is that you will be asked to do more nice things for other people.

8. You can be a generous, insightful, and thoughtful colleague, but that doesn't necessarily mean anyone you work with will notice if you're sad or disappointed.

9. Handwriting does not count.

10. Worrying about retaining water is only important if you are a boat.

11. A high IQ, EQ, SAT score, LSAT score, GRE score, MCAT score, et cetera, is proof merely that you have scored well on that test.

12. Just because you remember other people's birthdays doesn't mean they'll remember yours.

13. The fact that it is free does not necessarily mean it is okay to take as much as you want. Put back the mints, the matches, the tiny individual packets of salt and pepper, the postcards you'll never send, the straws (why on earth do you want straws?), the small cups, the plastic cutlery, the paper napkins, and the Sweet'N Low.

14. Just because the show is great does not mean it will stay on the air. To put it another way: the show does not always go on. Ask anybody who has done a pilot.

15. No one is interested in how many calories you consumed in any given time period.

16. The early worm gets eaten by the bird. But at least it doesn't talk about how many calories it consumed.

17. Being grateful—in and of itself—does not guarantee the continuance of the blessing. Saying "thanks" is not the same as saying "more," and the two should not be confused.

18. It is always fun until somebody puts out an eye.

19. Poor boys are better dancers than rich boys.

20. A good tailor, a good shoe-repair place, a good bakery, a good reading light, a healthy pet, and reliable phone service make life infinitely better.

21. Second wives usually get along with their mothers-in-law better than their husbands' first wives.

22. Your favorite colleague is not necessarily your best colleague.

23. Hiding your valuables does not guarantee they will not be stolen. Half the time you hide them in places where you yourself cannot find them the next time you search for them. This is not good. You end up stealing from yourself.

24. Only the truly innocent pay retail.

25. Eating fiber does not, in and of itself, make you morally superior to your peers.

26. The world is not static; tomorrow will not be like today no matter how well we plan.

27. If you feel you're overwhelming someone, consider the fact that he or she might simply be underwhelming you.

28. Not everybody looks better with highlights.

29. Just because you're good-looking doesn't mean everyone will find you attractive.

30. "Cuteness" and "perkiness" have a short shelf life in terms of life-partner personality traits.

31. There are more losers than winners at casinos and beauty contests.

32. "Power bars" do not contain actual power. These slabs of tar are good for those embarking on triathlons. Stop thinking that because you have to go to work in the morning you're ascending Everest; have a cup of coffee, a donut, and a banana, and take yourself less seriously.

33. The cream does not always rise to the top. (But coffee is still better than a power bar.)

34. Glasses do not make everyone look intelligent.

35. Not all accents are sexy.

36. Don't permit yourself to phone someone when you are actively crying. Wait until you're no longer in danger of gulping air before you dial.

37. Many people get to where they are by pretending to be somebody they're not.

38. If you repay injury with kindness, how will you repay kindness itself? By hitting those who are good to you over the head? It can get confusing if you mix up your friends and your enemies. The quality of mercy can be strained, despite what anybody says, and who needs strained mercy? Keep mercy for

those who actually merit it; it's yours, after all, and you don't have to spread it around like it's not valuable. You can end up cutting a vicious ex-lover all kinds of slack while hanging up on a perfectly good acquaintance who didn't, for example, RSVP in a timely fashion. Remember never to underestimate the delights of justice or the deliciousness of certain forms of mild revenge.

39. Most men are incapable of conversation. Most men engage in serial monologues.

40. There comes a point in every relationship when you either break up or form a permanent union. Either you'll see the person every day for the rest of your life or you'll never see him again. Decide which you really want to have happen before you have the showdown conversation deciding the outcome.

41. The experience of enjoying the company of a person you don't like is actually *much* worse than not enjoying the company of somebody you like.

42. Remember that in life, as in a taxi, the meter is always running. Make good use of the time you spend in transit.

43. Most people step on the brakes when a plane comes in for landing.

44. Who wants a boyfriend like a pet rabbit? At least a tomcat or a hound dog will give you a run for your money.

45. Men don't pay call girls for sex. They pay call girls for going directly home *after* sex.

46. Some people have a heart of gold. Be careful of these people. Like gold, their hearts can be bought by the ounce, and you can count on the price going up.

47. When you have daughters, you should save for weddings; when you have sons, you should start saving for bail.

48. Drink is the solvent many people use to break up their emotions. And their relationships. There's a reason the expression is "bottoms up!"

49. Certain people are entirely self-contained yet vulnerable, like an egg. Be wary if you find yourself in a basket among them.

50. Your enemy is not necessarily your rival and your rival is not always your enemy.

51. It is impossible to be aggressive and defensive at the same time. Even football players and generals know this. Decide which stance you're taking and stick to it.

52. Not everyone loves a parade.

32

YES, IT IS MY *REAL* COLOR,

SINCE I PAID FOR IT

I'm going through stupid hair trauma.

My adolescence was spent looking in the bathroom medicine cabinet mirror and taking the manicure scissors to my curls. This often occurred while I was weeping. No doubt part of that hair-cutting gesture depended on a fundamental lack of self-esteem that has followed me, like toilet paper stuck to my heel, through my life.

But at least some of it has to do with a girl's basic belief that if she cuts her hair, she can transform her face, her weight, her coloring, and her entire emotional environment.

Right now, I'm caught between various hair worlds. Why? Because my hair has been entirely white since I was in my thirties.

About three years ago, I decided to let parts of my hair stay white while I colored (translation: "dyed") the rest.

On a good day, this makes me look like Elvira, Queen of the Night. On a bad day, I look like Paulie Walnuts from *The Sopranos*. No, not like his sister—like Paulie.

Sure, some women look fabulous with their silver hair, but I doubt I'd look anything like Meryl Streep in *The Devil Wears Prada*. I fear instead that I would resemble Sophia from *The Golden Girls*.

I haven't seen my actual hair in six or seven years, because I've had it highlighted or colored since I saw gray. I've been red, brown, wheat, corn, and squash. Everything except zucchini. Now I'm letting it grow out. It looks like a glacier is gradually descending down my face.

Here's the other ridiculous Dippity-do quandary: I'm confused about how I look with my hair down versus my hair up. Last semester, I confronted twenty or so unsuspecting students as they walked into my office with: "Hair up or hair down?" They knew what I meant by the question—they'd witnessed my various stylings all semester. All but one kid said, "Hair up."

I was both shocked and disappointed. Without consciously realizing it, I discovered I'd always thought of myself as looking much better with my dark (okay, artificially dark) hair down around my shoulders. My great fear is that putting my hair up makes me look like a cross between Sybil, Basil Fawlty's wife on *Fawlty Towers*, and an extra from the Gem Saloon on *Deadwood*. (In my wildest dreams, putting my hair up made me look like Julie Christie from *McCabe & Mrs. Miller*, but given that I didn't look like her to start with, it was unlikely that putting in a scrunchy would precipitate that transformation.)

The true story is that my whole life I've used my hair to cover my face. Having really bad skin as a teenager made me want to draw a curtain around myself and remain hidden. My hair acted as nature's version of a paper bag. As a young woman, I used to wish that I had been born in a country where women were hidden—except for their eyes.

I no longer wish that.

But my belief that I look better with my hair fluffed out around my face—or, even better, covering my face—is still rooted in a basic fear of encountering the world without armor or a veil.

Like Janis Joplin, I always wanted to hide behind my hair. Like Lady Godiva, I used to think it was pretty sexy. Like Rapunzel, I thought it made me look like I was out of a fairy tale—and I fantasized that I (or someone else) might be able to use it as a means of escape.

When I try on clothes or even shoes, I always look in the store mirror and play with my hair, never mind that the gesture will have little effect on whether or not I look good in an Eileen Fisher jacket or a pair of Stuart Weitzman heels. Yet I can't keep how my hair looks separate from the rest of me. It's almost as if it belongs to somebody else and I'm wearing it like a hat.

(Several brave women I know have lost their hair because they've gone through chemo. Most of them have commented on the trauma of this event despite the fact that they have much bigger things to worry about. Some can't wait for their hair to grow back, while others have embraced a kind of Annie Lennox/Grace Jones minimalist approach. It's fascinating that something as apparently incidental as hair still commands attention, even when it's put into a larger, even more profound context.)

But what I've realized writing this is that almost everything that I've associated with hair has to do with other people—and that I should worry less about how I look than about the fact that I prowl the house with manicure scissors.

Maybe I should accept myself the way I am.

And keep it up.

33

WHO NEEDS A HUSBAND, ANYWAY?

Why was I not shocked to see a Reuters headline announcing "Most Single Japanese Women Want to Stay Unmarried"?

Why is it newsworthy, according to the international press syndicate, that "most single Japanese women prefer not to marry and believe they can live happily alone for the rest of their life"? New information, recently collected from a poll taken by one of Japan's conservative daily papers, points to a "trend among single women who no longer attach social stigma to choosing the single life."

Let's put it another way: if the headline read "Most Single Japanese *Men* Want to Stay Unmarried" would it be news? And, frankly, we can just leave out the whole national-identity business; how about a headline saying "Cute Successful Young Men Not Hurrying in Droves Toward Altar"?

That wouldn't be news, would it?

What makes the Tokyo report newsworthy, apparently, is the fact that the phrase "live happily alone" and the word "women" were linked.

In America—and, apparently, around the world—we traditionally expect women to want to be married. The theme song for women in relationships is Carole King's "Will You Love Me Tomorrow?" while the theme song for men in relationships is Bob Seger's "We've Got Tonight" (a title followed instantaneously by an invitation).

Even if we don't think of women wanting to *be* married, we at least think of them wanting to *get* married. Just as there are plenty of people who adore kittens but don't really like cats, there are plenty of girls who would love to be brides but don't really want to be wives. Whereas very few boys grow up looking forward to the day that they'll be a groom. There is no *American Groom* magazine. G.I. Joe does not have a little tux with a cummerbund; in fact, we know precious little about Joe's personal life. He's a don't-ask-don't-tell kind of doll. We only know that he has a job and his job is to kill other toys.

And while the idea of marriage is like the very air around us—unseen, full of pressures, and exerting influences we don't even realize—perhaps the younger generation is discovering that, unlike air, you can live without it.

Or maybe somebody simply explained that they could buy their own toaster ovens, blenders, and George Foreman Grills, thereby skipping the appliance-based early marriage syndrome. Young people have learned that they can amuse themselves in other ways: by learning a language, for example, or taking up a sport.

The news from Tokyo had been predicted, mind you: a 1953 issue of *Good Housekeeping,* one of the most widely read "ladies' magazines" of its day, ran a piece titled "This Is Why" arguing on behalf of early marriages. According to the author,

> being an older unmarried girl of [twenty-five or twenty-six has its] problems as well as its superficial advantages.
>
> As a career girl in your late twenties, you have been most probably able to surround yourself with certain material assets . . . to which you shortly become accustomed. Will you then be eager to marry a man who cannot keep you in your customary supply of worldly goods?

The only sensible answer to which is, of course, "What are you, nuts? No way."

Clearly the intention in 1953 was to pour fear into the heart of any young woman foolish enough to choose independence over dependence: after all, independence can be dangerously habit-forming. To make the subtext more explicit: if you find that you can live alone, why would you ever marry?

Is our estimation of marriage so low it collapses under the weight of any comparison with unmarried life?

"Better to marry than to burn," wrote Saint Paul in another backhanded compliment to marriage. Better, too, to marry than to be forced into frigidity. Women who did not marry were considered outcasts, expired goods, or bitter spinsters. The images we saw of these women made us shiver. (Shelley Winters once described a hotel room in Philadelphia as being "so cold, I almost got married.")

Remember Donna Reed's character in *It's a Wonderful Life*? During the part of the movie where Jimmy Stewart's character gets to see what the world would have been like had he never been born, he witnesses all sorts of tragedies: the death of his beloved brother, the alcoholism and ruin of his boss, and—horror of horror—the unmarried life of the Donna Reed character. It is one of the climaxes of the film: Jimmy Stewart realizing with misery and terror combined that had he never been born, this woman would now be not only single but also—gasp!—a librarian! He, therefore, decides that his life was meaningful, if only because he saved people from death, ruin, and the sheer misery of a single woman who is perpetually in circulation.

Those of us who have the sufficient good fortune to live with someone we love inside the context of a marriage should remember that there are other ways of living and loving.

Marriage isn't a disease; it isn't catching. You don't have to pass it on to everybody you know. Unlike a woman I once heard admit, "I've never been married, but I tell people I'm divorced so they are not scared of me," the Tokyo girls seem unapologetic and eager to be happy in their own lives whether or not those lives are shared.

Maybe that is indeed worth a headline.

34

WHY HAVE I NEVER HEARD A MAN SAY, "OH, THE NEXT MONTH IS GOING TO BE *REALLY* BUSY BECAUSE I'M GETTING READY FOR THE HOLIDAYS"?

Why do holiday preparations remains a secondary sex characteristic for females, similar to the ability to braid hair and remember birthdays?

Why is this burden placed on the narrow (although buff and fit) shoulders of women?

Is it chromosomal, built into DNA? Have females simply evolved the gift-wrapping gene?

Has survival of the fittest prepared us, and us alone, for the daunting task of hitting T.J.Maxx with a coupon for 15 percent off any regularly priced item?

Is it a skill honed by our cave-dwelling ancestors that leads us to purchase, by the crate, hand-forged votive candleholders embossed with the international sign for an environmentally safe world from a catalog? Why is it that most men don't even know what a votive candle *is*?

Only two X chromosomes could account for the creation of pomander balls by thousands of women who otherwise seem not to suffer from any grievous psychological ailment. I mean, can you just imagine giving the following instructions to any male of the species? "Use a toothpick to prick a hole in the skin of a piece of fruit such as an apple or orange. Then place a clove in the hole. Repeat until the entire fruit is covered with cloves. Next stick the tips of a wire hairpin into the fruit at the stem. Then roll the fruit in a dish of cinnamon. Place the fruit in a piece of cheesecloth. Twist the cheesecloth together around the hairpin. Use a piece of yarn to tie the cheesecloth onto the hairpin. Next tie a ribbon bow around the yarn. Allow the fruit to dry in a cool, dark place until the fruit hardens."

I don't even know where to begin in terms of gender specificity. It would be illegal in most states to force men to perform these tasks. If you told a boy that he had to make a gift for someone he loved out of rotting fruit, hairpins, and cheesecloth, he might find the concept intriguing—think of the possibilities in terms of making a mess, after all—but when he discovered that the process involved the systematic implantation of hundreds of cloves, he would plead his case to Child Protective Services.

At the holiday season, it becomes particularly apparent that all women, not only stay-at-home moms or naturally crafty types, are driven to express themselves through their holiday decorations. This is not always happy thing. There is, for example, a cultural craving for polymer clay. Apparently women across America are driven to create decorations through what sounds like the unnatural pairing of polymer clay and pasta makers. Perhaps we're seeing a generation who once enjoyed using the Play-Doh Fun Factory attempting to bridge the gap between something advertised on *Captain Kangaroo* and something exhibited in the Louvre.

And for the truly obsessive-compulsive crafter, there are die-cutters. In order to achieve a perfectly designed star, heart, or snowman shape, the use of scissors is no longer appropriate. Tools made especially for this onerous task are what the truly gifted crafter must use.

All of this pales in comparison to a need for "embellishments." Embellishments are the absolute rage. I think it has something to do with rubber stamps, but I'm not really sure. I was a little surprised to learn that rubber stamps are considered the accoutrements of the artistic. I thought when you said, "I'm just gonna rubber-stamp that," it meant that you paid no attention whatsoever; to rubber-stamp something was to dismiss it as quickly and generically as possible. Now, however, rubber stamps have been elevated to the place etchings used to hold, though I can't imagine any line of seduction beginning, "Would you like to come upstairs and see my rubber stamps?"

I can more easily imagine someone saying, "Would you like to come up and see my pomander balls?"

Enjoy the pre-holiday season. Light a votive candle for me.

35

IS THAT AN ANGEL ON MY SPARKLY STRAIGHTJACKET?

There I was, browsing in an upscale shop famous for its wine accessories (a fact that already indicates that I have *way* too much time on my hands and should do more volunteer work), and I found myself tempted to buy a diminutive Santa outfit. This tiny garment was designed to be slipped over a wine bottle on a festive occasion. I thought it would make a nifty holiday present.

"Honey," I called to my husband, who was across the sales floor seemingly enthralled by a chess set composed of shot glasses (another truly necessary seasonal item). "Come and look at this cute little costume for a bottle of Chablis!"

Let's say he was less enthusiastic. My husband's response can best be summed up as, "Sweetie, you've lost it. You really think any of our friends have on their wish list 'Clothes for Booze'?"

Is That an Angel on My Sparkly Straightjacket?

Why *do* we give what we give on the holidays? Why has the apparently generous, even jolly, opportunity to present objects of our affection with tokens of our tenderness turned into an unpardonably frantic set of tasks? When did the chance both to give and to receive morph into an anxiety-provoking situation along the line of a tax audit or the SATs?

Did the ritual of wrapping paper and tying bows begin as a way to disguise our astonishingly poor gift choices? Did putting stuff in boxes and then hiding the boxes spring from the deep embarrassment with which we regard our purchases once we're irrevocably committed to giving them? "Well, goodness knows Dad really *needs* this turbo-charged, Teflon-coated, battery-operated nose-hair clipper," you reassure yourself, "but I'll just put it in thirteen layers of tissue paper so that he won't be able to see it right away. I'll wrap the batteries in a separate box. He'll enjoy the surprise."

Like fun he will. Giving somebody a grooming device is just about as tactful as offering a stick of deodorant or a load of dental floss. And don't kid yourself: that the dental floss is gaily colored doesn't suddenly turn it into an appropriate present.

To the paranoid among us, of course, every cheerful gift box or glittering envelope can contain an insult. Let's say you decide to give your sweetheart a year's pass to the local gym. You know he's into lifting or you know she enjoys swimming, and so you decide that a membership to the facility with the best weights or the best pool will be your best bet.

This will guarantee that you are faced not with a buff and healthy partner but with a tense or teary one. "Ha, ha, don't you like the way I look?" the gift's recipient will chortle. This is a good time to move a little closer to the exit. "You think I need to work out more? Why didn't you get *yourself* one so we could go together? You think you're *perfect? You think you're looking just dandy?"*

Better to have bought Belgian chocolates. Or a Pinot Noir dressed as Kris Kringle.

I'm not sure whether it's better to give a rotten present or to get one. I've done both, so you'd think I could come up with an authoritative answer to this question. But it's a tough call. Here are the choices: was it more miserable to have been given at age twenty-one, by a boyfriend I adored, a copy of the book *Fowler's Modern English Usage* wherein my boyfriend marked every example, definition, and term he thought I needed to understand more fully (this was not a gift; it was a lesson plan), or to have given, to an old friend from college, a beautifully framed and enlarged photograph of herself? Sounds fine, right? Thoughtful, even? I'd had the privilege of snapping the picture a year earlier. I didn't realize that, in the space of time since I'd last seen her, my friend had undergone intensive "work" on her face as well as on her extended person. The new woman who unwrapped the gift resembled the mature woman in the photograph just about as much as I did. How could I, with my kindly meant gift from Kodak, hope to compete with a lady who'd given herself the gift of Botox? It wasn't like I was insulting her—I was simply unaware that she had one of those makeovers that cross over the boundary between plastic surgery and special effects. Trying to smile in thanks, she produced only a look so bitter and resentful it was the kind of expression ordinarily reserved for the loyal girlfriends of serial killers. Now we just send each other holiday cards. Not the family-photograph kind.

I've heard even scarier stories. My friend John's family was not exactly known for their sensitivity to the needs of their nearest and dearest: turning the cool age of thirteen, for example, John had his heart absolutely set on a snare drum, only to receive, instead, a gooseneck lamp wrapped in a snare-sized box. Thirty years later, there is still bitterness. He also reports having used gift inappropriateness as a barometer of family feeling. "I knew my parents were headed for divorce when all Dad got Mom one year was a turkey baster," John explains. "You wanted one of these, right?" John's father apparently said in response to his wife's incredulity. "Even if my mother needed a turkey baster in the kitchen, she realized at that moment what she *really* needed was a good lawyer on the phone."

Some of the best presents are not wrapped up or on any conscious wish list. When I was in graduate school, an elderly uncle showed up at my quark-sized New York apartment proclaiming that he carried, in a crumpled paper bag, "what every woman wants." It seemed unlikely. This uncle was at the phase of his life when he was prone to showing up with last week's paper under his arm because "it's always the same thing. What does it matter if the news is a little old?" Despite my initial skepticism, my uncle in fact made good on his promise: he handed me a full page of first-class stamps, five bags of subway tokens, and a bottle of Chanel No. 5. He saved me time, expense, trouble, provided necessities, and gave me something I never could have afforded to give myself.

There's another explanation for the rituals surrounding holiday gifts, one that has less to do with the presents and more to do with the future. Like a gift under the tree, the future is in sight but nevertheless cloaked by the unknown. It's hidden from us by the quotidian wrapping of the calendar, only to be unveiled at the precisely orchestrated moment of the new day. What's next could be everything we've always hoped for. Or it could be heartbreaking. Who knows?

The night before any big day—and tomorrow is one of the biggest—there is something young in us, something extravagantly curious about what is ahead. On Christmas Eve we breathe a collective deep sigh of both wistfulness and anticipation. Like a child about to ride a bike for the first time, we turn our heads to smile at what we leave behind even as we begin to contemplate what's ahead. If we're smart, we call upon all the courage we can manage and we take what's given to us with gratitude, with perspective, and with a spirit of understanding.

If we're very smart, we also keep the receipt.

I always noticed, when setting up the Christmas crèche under the tree as a kid, that Mary, Joseph, and baby Jesus were surrounded by friends instead of family. Three kings, some shepherds, a couple of angels—they were all part of the festive manger scene. There was, however, a noticeable absence of siblings, aunts and uncles, cousins, second cousins, and great-aunts.

There was little or no intimation of the substantial familial crowds we ourselves were likely to encounter at my grandma's house on the twenty-fifth of December.

As a child, I really *liked* that Joseph and Mary had welcomed friends and acquaintances rather than (or maybe in addition to) family into their big day. While we acknowledge our astonishingly good fortune in having a number of people for whom we care deeply (and yes, other family members are chief among them), we also choose to say, on the twenty-fifth of December: "It is all of you we count on during the darkest, briefest days and the longest, coldest nights. Here's to the meal in front of us, the good company around us, the hard times behind us, and the happiness ahead of us. We look forward to all that we will celebrate in the upcoming year, but alongside those times of joy we can also see glimpses of when we will call out so that you will lighten a burden, calm a racing heart, or wipe away a tear. We know you will listen to us and love us anyway."

That's what you want for the holidays: home. And home is where they love you even when they *really* know you, after all.

Having said that, however, I am horrified by the following aspects of the holiday season, all of which make me wish to put an X across "Xmas":

1. The remorseless cheer of holiday music that sticks in your brain like cotton candy, causing otherwise grown-up people to hum "Rudolph the Red-Nosed Reindeer" at inopportune moments such as during department meetings or sexual foreplay (events that rarely occur together, even in the most progressive of neighborhoods).

2. Toboggans and the idea that somebody might suggest I would like to take a ride on one, which I would not. I'll admit that when I was a kid I used to love riding down snowy hills outside

my junior high school on plastic lunch trays stolen from the cafeteria, but those days are long gone.

3. The prancing self-righteousness of those who do their holiday preparations early. These folks need to find a hobby that doesn't make the rest of us feel inadequate. A teacher who starts putting snowflakes on the classroom windows before Columbus Day, for example, needs to spend *way* less time at the Christmas Tree Shoppes.

4. Having to hear about the possibility of "lake effect snow" during the evening news and being given false hope of a day off when, in fact, it's just the evil manipulations of the local TV station to get us to watch their programming all evening.

5. Having to fit into festive holiday sweaters that are about as comfortable—and about as flattering—as a Goofy costume.

6. Brassy-tasting, alcohol-free eggnog, which tastes as if it has been made with runoff from "lake effect snow."

7. Wondering what to buy the twelve-year-old nephew who, when asked to provide a wish list of gifts, started off with "A brace of concubines."

8. Jack Frost nipping at any of my extremities.

9. Having to mutter, with a humble false smile, "No thanks, I was just browsing," approximately 1,345 times to poor, tired, and hungry salesclerks sporting bewildered expressions who dread my approach as much as I dread theirs. Also, they never know which department might have the brace of concubines I might be searching for.

10. My freakish need to watch Christmas-themed films when I know they will make me cry. If I see any character from *A*

Christmas Carol or even one of the loser-misfit toys from the old animated *Rudolph* I instantly burst into tears.

11. End-of-year work parties more accurately described as impromptu mating seasons. You want to give yourself the willies? Watch a couple of your less adorable colleagues tease one another about kissing under the mistletoe. Actually, dealing with co-workers for whom you have developed an almost electric aversion is the worst part of these events. You still have to be nice to them even when they are creeping you out by being all gooily friendly because it's "that time of the year." (This is especially difficult when it happens to coincide with "that time of the month.")

12. The profligate use of sparkles, sequins, glitter, and tinsel. Enough already. If you are over twenty-two, do not use any of these items on your person. Trust me on this one: it doesn't help and might actually hurt.

36

WHO'RE YOU CALLING SANTA'S BABY?

The Other Woman's favorite Christmas song is Eartha Kitt's "Santa Baby." After all, it's clearly not Mrs. Claus who's inviting Santa to hurry down her chimney and trim her tree.

The Other Woman sings with gusto, enjoying the lyrics that remind Santa about all the fellas she hasn't kissed—thus defining her as "good." But there's a little more anger every year, an emotion as pointed as a poinsettia but not as pretty. You can hear it most clearly when she gets to the line about wanting a "ring" ("I don't mean on the phone").

If she's over thirty-five, she probably suspects she isn't getting that ring.

Maybe she tells herself she doesn't want it: After all, she already has a full life and why clutter it up with a full-time relationship?

Where would she find the time, the energy, the metaphoric and literal space? She gets the best of him and his wife gets the rest.

That's her internal monologue and, for much of the time at least, the mantra soothes her.

But holidays make it harder to find a safe place in her head. It's as if the world conspires against her from Thanksgiving through New Year's Day. Any day with a parade, actually, is not one of her favorites.

What's she going to do in celebration of the season? Put a photograph of herself and her 500-count Egyptian sheets on a Shutterbug card and send it out with a warmhearted message?

Halloween is her holiday, with masks and disguises, with catsuits and pirate outfits. She's a shape-shifter, a plunderer, a thief, and she knows it.

Call her all the names you want, and you'll discover that she's called herself worse. It's not like you're telling her something she doesn't know. She's the backstreet girl, the booty call *in perpetuum*.

She's Jezebel. She's Little Suzy Homewrecker.

So she makes the round of holiday parties, makes cookies and makes pies, makes jokes and makes new friends. She makes nice. She is nice. It's not bad, but there's a blanked-out figure where the man she loves should be.

She can't call him; too risky. She can't e-mail him; anything in writing is out. She's tempted, at her worst moments, to drive by his house in order to catch a glimpse of him through the window when his home is brightly lit after dark. Is his car there? Is hers there—the other her? The wife?

Not "his wife" but "the wife."

The Other Woman thinks about his marriage as if he weren't part of the emotional equation, as if his own choices and desires didn't factor in.

She's met his wife. Of course she has.

Over the holidays there might be gatherings where they'll all meet by accident-on-purpose on her part, where she'll dash in perfectly dressed and pink cheeked from the cold and with the anticipation of seeing him, however briefly and publicly, and he'll stand next to his wife, awkwardly shifting his weight from foot to foot and wrinkling his forehead in an embarrassed grin as if to say, "You know how I feel, right?" He'll look about six years old, a kid who discovered where the toys were hidden long before they were wrapped and played with them without telling anybody.

If he told, then somebody might take the toys away because it wouldn't be fair. His sheepish look is undercut by a devilish grin. He shrugs his shoulders as if to say, "Okay, you caught me. But, hey, you know me inside out and I love you for it."

In the past she's always found that little-kid-with-a-secret-look endearing. But today she's less impressed. Maybe she looks at the wife, a woman more like herself than she'd care to admit. Usually she thinks of the wife as the woman who has everything and doesn't appreciate it, but today she looks restless, tired, over-worked, needy, and a little frantic around the eyes. She looks older, but then who doesn't?

Can this really be her rival? Is this the enemy she cries herself to sleep over on those nights when she can't convince herself that she has the best part of the deal?

Who're You Calling Santa's Baby?

During the holidays, the Other Woman goes for lots of long walks, to clear her head, to keep herself in shape, to get out into the world and out of herself. She walks by a rink and sees the skaters, singly and in pairs, moving with surprising grace. After watching for quite some time, almost mesmerized, she sees how one skater who'd been keeping up a lively pace slows, turns briefly to wave to her companion, and leaves the ice without faltering or looking back.

She thinks about how the only thing to do when you want to stop going in circles is stop.

"Think of all the fun I've missed," she sings, a line from "Santa Baby" that begins to take on new meaning as she walks back home.

37

WHY DO BAD THINGS HAPPEN

TO GOOD PEOPLE?

My grandmother's philosophy of life was this: whatever happens, happens for a reason.

She herself would have been hard-pressed to call this a philosophy. She didn't throw around too many four-syllable words in English, what with those nine children and the various complexities of tenement life during the depression. But maybe she thought about things while she did "piecework" at night, sewing the edges around buttonholes.

One of the ways she looked at life was to believe that—even if you could not understand it, even if it seemed like a tragedy or actually *was* a tragedy—everything happened for a reason. You might not understand the reason or accept it even if you understood it, but that was simply because your perspective was limited. "Bad luck could save you from worse luck," was her motto.

One of my early encounters with Grandma's philosophy came when I was about eight years old. I'd saved up money from birthdays and holidays, guarding dimes from cards sent by relatives who put coins in individual slots, making the currency seem miraculously multiplied. Through careful financial planning, I had about five or six dollars. It was enough money to go to the stores on the Avenue.

I wanted to own The Barbie Game by Mattel. The goal of this popular game was to get a dress, a part-time job, and a boyfriend. (NB: maybe there was also the hint that you should do well at school—I don't remember whether I'm inventing that part or not.) The winner, once these prizes were accumulated, was the first to go to the prom. This was the object of my desire and I looked forward to the possession of this toy the way a cat looks at a ball of wool: I could hardly wait to get my hands on it.

I would be kind enough to share my treasures with a select crowd. Two of my friends accompanied me to the toy store; I was as smug as if they constituted a royal entourage. The dusty, cluttered shelves of the small, old store contained all of life's riches. The Barbie Game was there in all its glory, and I held it reverentially, almost tenderly, as I approached the cash register.

Which is when I discovered that, in the couple of blocks between my house and the store, I had lost all my money. In tears and in a state of panic, I asked the nice man at the counter to hold the game for me, lest it be purchased by a more economically secure little girl, and my friends and I started searching the sidewalks for my lost fortune.

It was a busy Saturday. Streets were filled with people. One of those people had been lucky enough to look down and see a couple of bucks in the gutter and, naturally enough, picked it up. The money was gone.

Of course the money was gone.

I was inconsolable. My friends were disappointed but couldn't share my knife-edged sense of devastation. I had not only forfeited the cash and lost the chance to own The Barbie Game, but—insult to injury—I had wasted all the time and effort that went into saving up the money itself. My friends shuffled their feet, looked sad, and said good-bye on the corner.

My grandmother was alone in the house when I returned. I was sobbing, gritty and disheveled from scouring the city streets. She wiped my face with a damp dish towel in that rough way that grown-ups wipe the faces of little kids, attempting unsuccessfully to wipe away my despair along with the dirt, to remove the grief along with the grime. She sat me down at the big table and gave me a pignoli cookie and a glass of milk. Then she asked for an explanation.

Outraged and incredulous at the unfairness of it all, I explained what happened. I expected one of her enormous and enveloping hugs. I expected sympathy and consolation. I expected more cookies by way of reparations for the general injustice of the universe.

Instead of providing what I expected, however, Grandma shrugged and said, "Too bad you lost the money. But there must be a reason." She patted me on the head—no hug, no more cookies—and went back to doing the dishes.

This I could not accept; her response aroused in me a sense of indignity. I protested and she answered, calmly, as if explaining a fact that was embarrassingly self-evident, "Something bad would have happened if you'd got what you wanted. Be glad you didn't." When I asked how The Barbie Game could have damaged me, she said "Look, let's say you got the toy and you were so excited to show it to your little friends that you ran across the street without looking and you got hit by a car."

"Grandma," I said, somewhere between a sigh and a shout, "that wouldn't have happened!"

"How do you know, Miss Smarty-pants? Things happen. Bad things, sometimes. Maybe somebody," she looked heavenward and I knew she wasn't talking about the people on the second floor, "is looking out for you. You can't change it anyway. It is for the best."

I don't remember what I did for the rest of the afternoon, once that brief conversation was finished. I wish I could say it provoked a sudden change of heart. It did not. But now, almost forty years later, I reflect on my grandmother's words and I am astonished by her life: here was a girl who left Palermo when she was sixteen, sailed in the bottom of the boat (in steerage, where she was scared and sick and miserable) and moved to a new country, settled in a huge city she knew nothing about, not even how to speak its language. Yet she rolled up her sleeves and made life for herself and her family. The one thing about which she was certain was that there was—that there *had* to be—a reason for this turmoil.

There had to be a reason for the sense of loss she felt on those nights when she missed the old country, on afternoons when she longed to pick the figs right off the tree as she did in Sicily, or on cold days when she might have been tempted to barter her soul for sun and familiar voices.

I think The Barbie Game showed up for my birthday or Christmas and no doubt I was grateful. Somehow I doubt that my paternal grandmother had time to pick up a copy of *Candide* and be tickled by the inevitable comparison to the comic character of Pangloss, a figure who insists, "This is the best of all possible worlds."

38

LIKE, SERIOUSLY, IS ANYBODY MORE JUDGMENTAL THAN A TEENAGE GIRL?

Your average young female has ideas about the right way to look, act, speak; her standards are exact and unforgiving. Your average adolescent female makes Vlad the Impaler seem as all-embracing as Oprah.

And I'm not talking about other people here; I'm not discussing this topic from a completely disinterested, objective perspective. I'm talking about it as an erstwhile average young female.

How should I put this? I was not what you might call overwhelmingly nice as a young person. Want to know what's even scarier? When I was a kid, I was actually nicer than most of the other girls I knew.

I wouldn't have qualified as a Queen Bee—too nerdy—but I definitely liked a certain amount of buzz in my life. I was fascinated by the foibles and disasters of other people's lives. I looked at every-body and noticed every detail when they made a bad choice, acted in an embarrassing way, or screwed up generally. It made me breathe a little easier when examining my own flaws and missteps, of course, but it also provided a kind of entertainment usually associated with the gutter press.

Forget about finding a younger self who would welcome any-one and everyone, regardless of eccentricities or idiosyncrasies; forget about seeing myself as an innocent, sweet, naïve girl. My comments would make Joan Rivers at the Oscars seem generous. I wasn't exactly a miniature Mother Teresa. I was more of a minia-ture Nancy Grace.

When reading through my old diaries, I was horrified by what I wrote in the green-lined notebooks from sixth and seventh grade. These are, in essence, a catalog of judgments about everyone I'd ever met. This is not good news.

I never would have remembered how fierce I was in my as-sessments of those mortals who had the nerve to parade past my all-seeing eyes had I not written it down. Unapologetic, I flung judgments as if I were a Queen disappointed by her subjects. Those cheap little spiral notebooks are full of detailed, snarky, and vitu-perative commentary. Not exactly *The Princess Diaries*.

I was, for example, horribly embarrassed by my mother, a French-Canadian immigrant. Poor Maman; did she know what I was thinking? I made promises on nearly every page—promises to my-self that I would never be as awful as my mom. For example, my mother dared—dared!—to go out into the world wearing lipstick and eyebrow-defining pencil but *not* mascara. Can you believe it?

Actually my mother probably looked pretty hip, when I think about it, with her black raincoat, dark glasses, dark eyebrows, and scarlet lipstick. She sort of looked like Natasha from the Bullwinkle cartoon. But other mothers had dyed-blond hair in beehive hairdos. They wore pale peach lipstick. They wore huge fake eyelashes, which might have made them look as if they had giant spiders crawling over their eyeballs, but at least they were making, well, an effort. My mother was just going her own way, doing what she wanted to do. In my Queendom, such independence was improper.

I used to walk ten paces behind her so that nobody would guess we were related.

And my teachers? They came under scrutiny at least as careful— and twice as exacting.

Not all my teachers, of course, just the lady ones.

The male ones were not even worth examining (except for Mr. Frisco because he was cute—his was the only math class in which I ever did well). Male teachers were so few as to be considered sui generis; if they sported the same checkered jackets and light blue shirts, the same gray pants, the same brown shoes, then they had merely set their own incomparable styles.

But if a lady teacher wore the same dress twice in a week, we considered her either dotty or slutty. Why on earth would she do that? Was she too lazy to get her clothes cleaned or did she just leave the dress at her (giggle, snort) boyfriend's place the last time she spent the (giggle, shhhh) night there? Surely she spent as much time as we did picking out clothes for the week? Surely she knew we examined her from her toes (were the shoes new or worn down? were her stockings the old-lady opaque kind or the sheer ones?) to the top of her head (does she color her hair? does she use curlers? did she skip the wash and use Psssssst instead?).

If a teacher had a crooked tooth, lingering dandruff, or unsightly sweat stains (as if there are "sightly" ones . . .), then that eclipsed all other data. In my junior high, one teacher with a droopy eyelid became known as "Dead-Eye Donna." Even when she won a considerable sum on a lottery, we didn't change her nickname to "Rich Donna" or "Lucky Donna" or anything else vaguely flattering. She was "Dead-Eye" forever (she retired early).

I promised myself that if I became a teacher, I'd always look perfect. Now that I am a teacher, I just want to look clean. More or less.

If there's anything to karma, I'm in big trouble. The hallway to hell will be lined with gum-chewing little—and not so little—girls. And, for my sins, I'll be there without a friend, without a mirror, without mascara, and within sight of a kid who's writing everything down in her notebook.

39

TAKING YOUR ACT ON THE ROAD

After having completed a couple of weeks of traveling, I thought I would pass on the following hard-won information.

Worst Things About Traveling

1. Ordering "New York Style" pizza south of the Mason-Dixon Line (already a mistake) and ordering it with anchovies. The pizza turns out to be a four-inch slab of undercooked dough or, even worse, pita bread. The anchovies seem to be, on close examination, salted nostrils.

2. Being told to "make sure you fold the maps properly" by certain (male, always male) drivers, as if you were suddenly going to crumple the maps into tight rolls of paper or tear them into confetti for the sheer joy of making the driver unhappy.

3. Carrying postcards with you that you didn't buy until late in the trip, didn't write until even later, and that you will find stamps for only after you return home. (Entrepreneurs: Sell already-stamped local postcards from tourist locations. You will make so much money, it will be a sin. I will be first on line.)

4. Remembering that every day has its own continental divide and knowing that certain hours flow toward the morning and others go toward the night, just as after a certain point in your life there are years that connect you back to your youth while others move you along toward your death. Another way of putting this is that it's best to secure a good hotel room before noon.

5. The fact that you can never tell which TV stations are which on the hotel television; it doesn't matter if they write them out on a card and place the card conveniently next to the remote. Nobody reads the card. You sit on the bed, without taking off your shoes, and you flip until you find a station you recognize. In Indiana or certain counties within Minnesota, this can take hours.

6. The fact that, according to unnerving studies documenting the transmission of truly disgusting germs, TV remote-control devices are the ickiest part of any hotel room, even though nobody takes off their shoes when flopping down to turn on the television. This business about germs is saying something, when you think about it, especially if you remember that video about how nobody ever washed the glasses in hotel bathrooms ever.

7. You'll end up watching crap no matter what. You'll end up watching a made-for-television movie starring Bruce Springsteen's first wife on a station called Fallopian Tube because you can't be bothered to watch anything else.

8. Freezing or scalding showers: it is simply impossible to control water temperature accurately in a hotel. And when you do, finally, get the temperature even vaguely right, the person in the next room decides to shower and the water—as if possessed by the spirit of Norman Bates—maniacally freezes or scalds you.

9. Tollbooths that don't tell you how much money you need to pay until you are in the tollbooth itself, whereupon, presumably, the personnel can assess how much you can afford.

10. Forgetting to bring a book. There's not much to do in a lot of places after, say, eight o'clock on a weeknight. And most nights are weeknights, especially west of the Mississippi.

Best Things About Traveling

1. Discovering local cuisine. And the fact that Immodium can be purchased nationwide at most retail outlets.

2. Watching the odometer turning over to a rounded number.

3. Discovering ATMs that don't charge additional fees.

4. Finding out that the weather is lousy at home. This is the reason when, given a copy of *USA Today,* all readers instantly turn to the page listing the meteorological conditions of their state of residence. It is not, you can be sure, so that they'll know everybody's enjoying the sunshine and cool breezes back in

the neighborhood. People are secretly hoping for typhoon-like conditions, only with frost.

5. The fact that on a daily basis somebody else changes your sheets and towels.

6. The offer of multiple wake-up calls.

7. Finding a nice shrine with a good gift shop.

8. Adorable tiny souvenirs, locally crafted, incredibly cheap, that pack easily. Too bad these do not exist.

9. Figuring out vanity plates ("Pump FE"; "2 Gd 4 U").

10. Kids who wave from the back window. This is especially good if you can pass the car after a few miles, because even extreme cuteness gets old after forty-five minutes and besides, you don't want to end up on the Predators List by accident.

Tips on How to Make Traveling Better

1. Bring your own attractive, sturdy, disposable paper cups. Remember that trees are a renewable resource, but that some germs are forever (see "Worst Things About Traveling," no. 6).

2. Bring your own sparkling water. Most of America doesn't know from seltzer.

3. Make sure someone you love and trust checks in on your house and leaves you reassuring messages to say everything is fine at home.

4. Buy all the trinkets you want and worry about what to do with them later. The same advice does not apply to major furnishings.

5. If you're unhappy with service or the room at the hotel, ask them nicely to make it better. They usually will, and it is bet-

ter than stewing in anger and frustration. Ask for extra pillows and tip the person who brings them.

6. If you're happy with somebody who greets you, cheers you,
   serves you, welcomes you, helps you, let him or her know.
   Let that person's *boss* know, too, with one of those cards they
   always have at the front desk—or write a note at the restaurant for the manager. In the hospitality industry, compliments
   are taken seriously.

7. Don't worry about folding the maps perfectly; just do it as
   well as you can. If necessary, new maps can be purchased. You
   are neither Lewis nor Clark. Besides, a truly annoying traveling companion can be replaced by a GPS.

8. Eat the chocolate left on your pillow, if you're fortunate enough
   to be awarded chocolate. Unlike tiny toiletries, the little squares
   of chocolate don't travel well.

9. Learn how to sleep fast—if we can speed-read, why not speed-
   sleep?

10. Think how wonderful it will be to be safe and happy in your
    own bed once you get home. My favorite poem to be recited
    in anticipation of returning home was written by William James
    Lampton and goes like this:

Same old slippers,
Same old rice,
Same old glimpse,
Of paradise.

And remember—you can bring your own slippers with you.

40

BABES IN POLITICS LAND

I've thought long and hard about the women in the 2008 election cycle and what I'd like to say to them if I got to spend some time at a spa in Arizona with Cindy McCain, browse the J.Crew catalog online with Michelle Obama, browbeat a few men in the Senate with Hillary Clinton or, if I'm lucky, shoot a few moose with Sarah Palin. You know, even though I love them, and God knows I'm not bitter, there are a few things I would be compelled to say. What woman wouldn't? I've narrowed down my list and would love to hear what you think. Write to me at ginabarrecaforpresident2012.com (sorry, Sarah . . .).

If I were Cindy McCain, I would:

1. Give up on the dye bottle and spend more time browsing the racks at Eileen Fisher.
2. Have a cheeseburger every once in a while; for God's sake, social X-rays went out with the heyday of Judith Leiber minaudières.
3. Throw the old guy over, channel my inner cougar, and give Prince Harry a call.

I'd like to tell Michelle Obama to

1. Raise that prominent chin even higher as if to say, "Who're *you* looking at, exactly? And so what if I *do* resemble Jay Leno?" You're not going to disguise it, after all, and it's a great way to make your way into a room.
2. Wear some seriously bright colors and give Cindy McCain a run for her beer money; enough with the earth tones and Jackie jewelry, and don't ever, ever go near a pillbox hat, even as a joke.
3. Keep Barack in line by reminding him that all of Hillary's former supporters only voted for him because they think *you'll* make a terrific president one day.

As for Hillary, I'd have to be candid and say:

1. Hillary, you know I adore you more than lasagna Bolognese, but, Hillary, pantsuits really *are* just one element of a woman's wardrobe.

2. Darling, and I say this with as much love as possible, you are, without bringing up any names or assigning blame to any man no matter how well known he might be, simply one of those "women who love too much."

3. Only because we're so close do I dare even raise this point, sweetie, but do you think you could stop referring to women in power as "cracks" in the glass ceiling? It's such an infelicitous metaphor, don't you think?

And if I were lucky enough to go moose hunting with Sarah Palin, I'd have to pose these questions:

1. Okay, miss, it's just you, me, and the moose. You're a well-groomed, vibrant young woman. How thrilled were you—and speak candidly, please—about the whole world calling you . . . "Grandma"?

2. Quick, Sarah, pick an answer to the following question: You believe violent, unemployed youths should: a. Receive more education; b. Receive early training in technological skills; c. Marry your daughter.

3. Is the horrible rumor true, Sarah, dear? You know, the one that nobody wants to discuss while you're in the room but which even those closest to you won't deny. Is it true, Sarah, that you were the one who *really* shot Bambi's mother? It's not that I'm bitter. I'm just asking.